THE **2 0 1 4**

Thumbnail

Media Planner

The 12th annual *Thumbnail Media Planner* is once again bigger and better than ever…with updated media/marketing content, more data for digital media plus the additions of market and media data for emerging markets—Baby Boomers, Hispanic market, as well as the Asian American, and African American markets.

The purpose of the *Thumbnail Media Planner* is to provide a quick source of basic marketing and media data for advertisers, AEs, media planners and buyers, entrepreneurs, international advertisers who wish to advertise in the USA, and academics who wish to use the Planner as a real world media planning tool.

By providing important market and inter-media information, the *Planner* can help users understand the U.S. market and the market and media landscape, immediately answer many questions in meetings (saving time and cost) as a consequence, establish professional credibility, estimate preliminary budgets, evaluate new ideas and approaches in the early stages of the planning process.

Use the Planner to develop initial cost estimates and evaluate media alternatives. The Planner is not a substitute for rigorous research, planning, and precise cost estimating when more precision is needed.

Note: While we have attempted to forecast realistic media costs for 2014, actual pricing will be a function of supply and demand, i.e., if advertiser demand for media time and space increases in 2014, prices will likely rise. If the market grows even softer because advertisers are cutting back, prices may decrease further.

THE 2014 Thumbnail Media Planner

Copyright 2014

by

2020:Marketing Communications LLC

ISBN-13: 978-1493590254   ISBN-10: 1493590251

Disclaimer

This publication is intended to provide accurate and authoritative information. However, we cannot guarantee the accuracy of data in the scores of sources utilized. The Thumbnail Media Planner is sold with the understanding that the author is not engaged in rendering any legal, accounting, or other services. If such advice is needed, the services of a competent professional should be sought.

2020: Marketing Communications LLC

P.O. 82476, Rochester, MI 48308

Email:ThumbnailPlanner@aol.com

TABLE OF CONTENTS

1

Market Facts

A Quick Marketing Reference

*A quick reference for population and marketing statistics,
Retail sales data, marketing communications and
advertising expenditures, media efficiency benchmarks and
2020's exclusive media market outlook for 2014.*

USA Population

Global Population Projections (Millions)

REGION	1990	2000	2011	2013E
World Population	5278	6081	6347	7000
USA Population	249	281	293	315
USA % Increase	--	13.1	4.3	5.5
USA % World	4.7	4.6	4.6	4.4

Source: U.S. Census, ASU Seidman Research Institute, 2002-2005

USA Population Demographics (Millions)

Census Data	1990	2000	2005	2010	% Ch. Vs '90
Total Population	249	282	295	308	24.1
Households	92	105	110	117	25.0
Families	65	72	77	78	24.6
Males	121	138	145	152	25.6
Females	128	144	150	157	22.7
Age 6	19	20	20	20	10.5
Under 18	63	72	66	83	1.6
18+	186	209	215	219	26.3
18-34	70	66	67	62	(2)
35-54	63	72	85	86	36.5
55+	52	59	63	76	50.0
White*	200	229	237	224	22.5
Black	30	36	38	39	33.3
Asian/Islands	7	18	20	17	228.5
Hispanic Origin	22	36	42	50	118.1
Northeast	51	54	56	57	11.8
Midwest.	60	65	67		11.6
South	85	103	110	115	35.3
West	53	66	69	72	35.8

Source: U.S. Census.   *Includes whites of Hispanic origin

More Demographics

U.S. Adults

	TOTAL ADULTS	MEN	WOMEN
# US ADULTS (MM)	221.8	107.4	114.5
MARITAL SATUS			
Single	24.0%	26.2	21.9
Married	56.6	59.5	53.9
Divorced/Sep.	19.4	14.3	24.3
HH INCOME			
< $20K	12.9	9.9	15.9
20-29.9K	9.5	8.7	10.2
$30- 39.9K	9.0	8.8	9.3
$40K+	68.5	72.4	64.6
$50K+	59.9	63.7	58.4
$75K+	40.9	43.9	38.0
EDUCATION			
Did not Grad H.S.	13.2	14.0	12.5
U.S. Grad	32.4	32.4	32.3
Some College	20.9	19.9	21.8
College Grad+	26.9	27.2	26.7

Source: SMRB

2013 USA Household Statistics (Millions)

	HH	% US
Total HH	117	100
TV Households	116	99
Multi Set HH	94	72
HD TV	47	41
Any Cable/DBS	104	90
Satellite TV	33	28
Digital Cable	51	44
DVD Player	101	88
Broadband (P2+)	--	64
DVR	37	32
Mobile Phone User13+	223	--
HH w/PC	81	73

Source: Nielsen, US Statistical Abstract

Top 30 Markets (DMAs) in USA

- Geographic markets vary widely in size and buying power
- Selection and weighting of markets are key decisions

Rank	DMA	% TV HH	Retail $/HH	% Ch.	Buy Power
1	New York	6.8	$32.8	17.7	7.8
2	Los Angeles	5.0	37.7	28.2	5.6
3	Chicago	3.1	27.8	16.8	3.5
4	Philadelphia	2.7	36.6	13.1	2.8
5	San. Fran/SJ	2.3	41.7	31.7	3.1
6	Boston	2.2	41.6	24.5	2.6
7	Dallas/FW	2.1	39.8	29.8	2.4
8	Washington DC	2.0	33.4	17.4	2.3
9	Atlanta	1.8	38.2	25.3	1.9
10	Detroit	1.8	39.9	22.8	1.9
11	Houston	1.7	36.2	28.9	2.0
12	Seattle/Tacoma	1.6	37.5	35.9	1.9
13	Tampa/St Pete	1.5	31`.4	17.8	1.3
14	Minneapolis/ SP	1.5	43.6	28.7	1.7
15	Cleveland	1.4	33.9	18.8	1.3
16	Phoenix	1.4	39.5	30.0	1.5
17	Miami/FL	1.4	35.4	11.8	1.4
18	Denver	1.3	38.3	25.9	1.4
19	Sacramento	1.2	33.6	31.5	1.2
20	Orlando	1.1	34.2	19.2	1.1
21	Pittsburgh	1.1	28.8	9.8	1.0
22	St Louis	1.1	33.3	17.8	1.0
23	Portland, O	1.0	39.5	24.9	1.0
24	Baltimore	1.0	33.2	21.0	1.0
25	Indianapolis	1.0	35.1	19.3	1.0
26	San Diego	.9	37.8	33.2	1.0
27	Hartford/NH	.9	34.2	12.8	1.0
28	Charlotte	.9	34.1	23.1	.8
29	Raleigh/Durham	.9	32.9	20.3	.8
30	Nashville	.8	35.4	30.97.8	.8

Source: TVB, Claritas, projected 5-year growth in sales **Table reads:** *New York DMA is 6.8% of total US households, has an average $32,500 retail sales per household with a projected 17.7% growth rate and a Sales Management Buying Power Index of 7.8—higher than its 6.8 share of households*

Retailer Sales by Segment
(Trillions)

- Total 2011 Retail Sales up an estimated 8.1% (Census, 1st 9 mo.)
- Winners: Gas stations and non-store retail
- Losers: Furniture. Department stores, electronics & appliances, general merchandise

	2011*	%Ch.
Total Retail Incl. Food Service	**$3,445**	**8.1**
Motor Vehicle & Parts Dealers	617	10.4
Auto & Other Motor Vehicle	556	10.9
Furniture/Furnishings	65	1.0
Building Materials/Supply Dealers	226	5.8
Food & Beverage	455	5.6
Gas Stations	403	19.5
Sporting Goods/Hobby/Books/Music	62	5.8
Department Stores	126	-0.9
Electronics & Appliances	70	-
Food & Beverage	436	2.3
Health & Personal	204	5.2
Clothing/Accessories	156	5.9
General Merchandise	447	3.5
Eating & Drinking	369	5.5
Non Store Retail	280	13.2

Seasonality of Retail Sales

% of Bi-Monthly Sales by Retail Category

CATEGORY	JF	MA	MJ	JA	SO	ND
Bldg Supply	13	17	19	18	17	15
Clothing	12	16	16	16	16	22
Computer	18	17	16	14	17	18
Department	13	15	16	16	16	24
Drug	15	16	17	16	16	19
Eat/Drink	15	17	17	17	17	17
Furniture	15	16	16	17	17	19
Grocery	15	16	17	17	17	18
Appliances	15	16	18	17	17	19
Auto	16	18	18	18	16	15
Electronics	16	15	14	16	15	25
Sport Goods	13	16	16	18	15	21

Geography of Retail Sales
Category Development Index

	Auto Dealers	Grocery	Eat/ Drink	Computer Equip	Dept. Stores
New York	79	117	106	109	74
Los Angeles	109	108	102	133	118
Chicago	85	94	113	172	134
Philadelphia	102	121	102	143	116
Dallas/FW	114	75	110	82	59
San Francisco	73	139	121	137	59
Atlanta	194	97	107	82	83
Boston	99	137	137	118	92
Houston	118	99	93	80	78
Phoenix	117	102	99	165	100
Detroit	103	80	74	74	90
Minneapolis	94	102	103	116	146

Source: TVB/US Census

Table Reads: Per capita sales at automotive & parts dealers in New York is below average (79% of the national average).

MARCOM Spending Trends
(Billions $)

- No ad industry growth since 2000
- Traditional Media declining, digital media growing
- Internet may pass television before 2020
- Winners: Internet, Event Marketing, Product Placement

	2000	2010	2013E	Index '13 vs.'10
Advertising	**$234**	**$267**	**$197**	**74**
Traditional Media	$207	$208	$151	73
Product Placem't	1	3	4	133
Movie Screen	1	1	.7	70
Custom Media	NA	NA	13	NA
YP/Directories	11	12	8	67
Event Mktg/Sponsorships	13	17	20	118
Online	**$8**	**$26**	**$41**	**195**
CPC	.8	12	20	167
Display	4	6	7	117
Rich & Video	.2	3	5	167
Mobile	NA	NA	3	++
Social	NA	NA	2	++
Other	3	5	4	80
Promotion	**306**	**335**	**324**	**97**
Trade	$176	$188	$170	90
Consumer	130	147	154	105
PR, incl WOMM	**$4**	**$5**	**$6**	**120**
GRAND TOTAL	**$552**	**$633**	**$568**	**90**

Source: Jack Myers media forecasts, Magna Global, Kantar, 202

Advertising Expenditure Trends Traditional Media

- Television spend, led by cable, is projected to grow 5% in 2013, continuing as largest medium in terms of ad spend
- Online spending should increase another 55-20%+, led again by search with fast growing small volume areas of mobile, social, and video
- Print, especially newspapers, will continue to decline slightly in 2013 vs. 2012

Medium	2012	2013E	Index
Television	**$61,183**	**$63.900**	**105**
Network TV	13,583	13,400	99
National Cable	23,800	26,200	110
Spot TV/Local	20.800	21,400	103
Syndicated	1,800	1,600	90
Spanish	1,200	1,300	108
Radio	**15.600**	**16,000**	**103**
Network	1,200	1,200	100
Spot/Local	14,400	14,800	103
Newspapers	**21,300**	**19,600**	**92**
National	900	800	89
Local	20.400	18.800	92
Magazines	**15,900**	**15.400**	**97**
Directories	**5,400**	**4,900**	**91**
Direct Mail	**21,500**	**20,900**	**97**
FSI	**2,000**	**2,100**	**105**
Outdoor	**6,900**	**7,200**	**104**
Online*	**36,000***	**41,000***	**114***
TOTAL W/ONLINE	**$185,783**	**$191,000**	**103**

Source: Magna Global, 2020:Marketing Communications LLC estimates

Top 50 National Advertisers – 2011

	Advertiser	Category	Ad $ (MM)	% Ch v. '09
1	Procter & Gamble	CPG	$4610	-18
2	AT&T	Utility	2980	-7
3	General Motors	Auto	2860	-17
4	Verizon	Communications	2450	-19
5	American Express	Financial Svs.	2220	+63
6	Pfizer	Pharma	2120	+1
7	Walmart	Retail	2050	+1
8	Time Warner	Media	2040	+9
9	J&J	HH Products	2020	-2
10	Walt Disney	Entertainment	1930	-2
11	JPMorgan	Financial Svs.	1910	+43
12	Ford Motor Co	Auto	1910	+30
13	Comcast	Media	1850	+4
14	Sears Holding	Retail	1770	+5
15	Toyota Motor Co.	Auto	1730	+35
16	Bank of America	Financial Svs.	1550	--
17	Target	Retail	1500	+31
18	Macy's	Retail	1410	+2
19	Sprint	Phone	1400	-7
20	Unilever	CPG	1370	--
21	Anheuser-Bush InBev	Brewer	1350	-8
22	Berkshire-Hathaway	Investment	1340	+17
23	News Corp	Media	1310	+18
24	JC Penney	Retail	1310	--
25	McDonalds	Fast Food	1290	+4.4
26	Fiat	Auto	1160	+75
27	U.S. Government	Various	1100	+7
28	Honda Motors	Auto	1060	+12
29	Nestle	CPG	1050	+10
30	Kohls	Retail	1010	+3
31	Kraft	CPG	1000	+15
32	PepsiCo	CPG	1000	+2
33	GlaxoSmith	Pharma	1000	--
	Advertiser	Category	Ad $ (MM)	% Ch v. '09
34	General Mills	CPG	986	+16

35	Viacom	Communications	960	+9
36	Microsoft	Web Technology	926	17
37	Merck	Pharma	921	-28
38	Sony	Electronics	892	-2
39	Nike	Apparel	887	--
40	Capital One	Financial Svs.	877	+58
41	Nissan Motor Co.	Auto	867	+37
42	Eli Lilly	Pharma	857	+14
43	SABMiller	Brewer	841	-9
44	DeutscheTelekom	Telecomm	820	+14
45	Yum Brands	Fast Food	797	+2
46	Lowes	DIY	778	+5
48	AstraZeneca	Pharma	773	+9
48	Home Depot	DIY	768	-4
49	Coca Cola	CPG	758	+5
50	Progressive	Insurance	743	+58

Advertising-Sales Ratios
Selected Sectors

Sector	Ad-Sales Ratio	% Ad Growth	% Sales Growth
Consumer Prod.	7.4	10.4	8.8
Health Care	3.1	5.9	7.7
Retail	1.7	3.9	4.7
Financial Svs	1.3	1.8	.6
Transport/Travel	1.9	5.7	4.4
Services*	2.9	3.5	8.0
Wholesale	.4	3.9	9.2
Avg. Sector	**2.0**	**2.7**	**5.5**

Source: Advertising Age/Schoenfeld Estimates

Using A/S Ratios - Examples

- A/S ratios are used to help establish budgets and compare spending rates to completion
- To calculate a budget using an A/S ratio, multiply sales dollars times the A/S ratio as shown below:

Sales	**$100,000,000**
A/S Ratio	**x .074**
Resulting Budget	**$7,400,000**

- You may wish to compare your A/S ratio to those of your competitors. To calculate an A/S ratio, divide budget by sales as shown below:

Budget	**$7,400,000**
Sales	**$100,000,000**
A/S Ratio	**.074**
Percent	**7.4%**

Number of Media Outlets

Medium	Number of Outlets	Source
Television Stations	**1391**	**TVB**
VHF	**356**	
UHF	**1025**	
Cable Networks	**535**	**CAB/Media Post**
National	**81**	
Regional News	**27**	
Regional Sports	**13**	
Magazines	**19,419**	**Directory of Mags.**
Consumer	**6734**	
Business	**12,685**	
Newspapers	**8974**	
Morning	**850**	
Evening	**570**	
Sunday	**850**	
Weekly	**6704**	
Outdoor Locations	**406,000**	**Media/Adv. Bk.**
30 Sheet Locations	**210,000**	
8 Sheet Locations	**140,000**	
Bulletin Locations	**56,000**	
Radio Stations	**10,754**	**RAB**
Country	**2088**	
News/Talk	**1375**	
Oldies	**684**	
Adult Contemporary	**625**	
Hispanic	**789**	
Websites	**182,000,000**	**Netcraft**

Consumer Media Behavior
How Consumers Spend their Media Time

- About half of time spent with media is spent watching television
- Listening to radio is second most time consuming
- Internet garners third most time, but only slightly more than 10% of time spent watching TV
- Everything else is distant runner up to radio which still appears to play an important role in peoples' lives

Hours Spent/Year

Media Activity	2010	2009	Index
Watching Television	1730	1693	102
Listening to Radio	654	744	88
Internet (Pure Play)	202	181	112
Recorded Music	130	172	80
Newspapers	152	169	90
Out of Home	134	133	100
Magazines	113	128	89
Video Games	99	107	93
Books (Consumer)	95	104	91
Home Video	55	61	90
Mobile (Pure Play)	35	21	167
Yellow Pages	10	11	91
Books (Educational)	8	8	100

Source: Veronis, Suhler, 2009, 2010

Consumer Media Behavior
Media Multi-Tasking

- Considerable multi-tasking with other media while watching television especially with computer/internet media
- Also, a third of respondents read while watching TV
- Multi-Tasking has a dual effect on TV viewing: on the one hand it can reduce the attention levels paid to programs and commercials vs. the word of mouth effect, e.g.:
- Social television will likely play a growing role as people send tweets, Facebook messages about the programs they are watching.

Multi-Tasking Behavior	Female	Male	Total
Read magazine or newspaper while watching TV	NA	NA	33%
Use PC while watching TV	NA	NA	59
Use smartphone while watching TV	NA	NA	40
Use tablet while watching TV	NA	NA	42
Check email during TV programs	60%	59%	60
Check email during commercials	60	59	59
Surf for unrelated info during programs	46	46	46
Surf for unrelated info during comm'ls	44	46	45
Visit social network site during programs	48	35	42
Visit social network site during comm'ls	47	36	42
Check sports scores	17	44	30
Look up info about programs	28	30	29
Look up info about an ad	17	21	19
Look up coupons deals related to an ad	15	12	13

Source: Nielsen, 2012 Entertainment, Media & Advertising Market Research Handbook

2014 Media Market Outlook

Assumptions

- Media prices in 2013 will be affected by 2013 spending benchmarks and perceived demand for time/space.
- In 2012, demand for advertising media was driven by anemic business results and forecasts, and also by "OTOs"-- the Olympics and elections-- which, short term, caused demand to exceed to supply of time short term but not long term
- When demand for ad time exceeds supply of time available, prices typically increase, depending on outlook. In 2013, there were no large short term impacts on supply because the Olympics and elections were over.
- In 2014, media costs in will be driven by the economy and how much ad spending companies will commit based on their objectives and level of economic confidence.
- The re-election of President Obama and the implementation of his health care bill will likely play a role in affecting the demand side for years to come. On the one hand, If the economy improves modestly as some "experts" predict, demand, ad budgets, and pricing would likely increase.
- In contrast, some believe that Obamacare will result in lower investments, employment and wages to offset higher health care costs which may cause the economy to falter, reduce demand for goods and services and advertising/marketing.
- At this time, assuming slow economic growth continues in 2013-2014 with relatively high unemployment and uncertainty on government regulations and taxes, the impact of health care legislation on business' ability to operate and invest, and so on, makes media forecasts difficult to forecast with any precision.

NET-NET   We are looking for a slightly brighter outlook for the media economy in 2013-2014, probably in the neighborhood of +5% total, +1-2% for network TV and +8-10% for internet.

Media Efficiency Benchmarks

2011-2012 CPM Comparisons

Medium	Men	Women
Network Television :30		
Early Morning	$19.50	$12.50
M-F Daytime	--	8.50
Early News	14.50	11.50
Prime Time	30.00	25.00
Late Night	25.00	22.00
Spot TV		
Daytime	--	$8.75
Early Fringe	12.00	10.00
Late Fringe	15.00	13.00
Cable Network :30		
Prime Time (avg.)	$20.00	$16.00
Radio		
Network :30	22.00	21.00
Spot :60	12.00	12.75
Magazines (P4C)		
Mens'	$30.00	--
Newsweeklies	21.00	--
Mass	19.00	12.00
Women's Fashion	--	17.00
Women's Service	--	15.00
Newspapers (1/4 page)	$65.00	$75.00
Outdoor (30 sheet)	$4.00	$4.50
Internet		
Banners/Display	$3.50	$3.50
Range	$1.00	$15.00+

*Impressions based on "interested" surfers theoretically "exposed" to banner ad
CPMs vary widely by product category
Source: 2020 estimates. Data shown as general benchmarks; actual CPMs will vary
depending on specific media vehicles.

2
Television

The Television Marketplace in 2013-14

A synthesized media planning reference for network, spot, and cable television for the 2013-2014 broadcast year. Data on audiences, costs research alerts, with historical CPM benchmarks are included along with 2020's exclusive TV market outlook for 2014.

Television

Advantages

- 98% reach potential, including upscale demographics
- Exposure frequency opportunity
- Sight/Sound/Motion and intrusiveness can increase message impact
- High geographic flexibility (national, regional, DMA, cable systems)
- Further targeting flexibility via selection of dayparts, programs, markets

Disadvantages

- High cost to achieve effective reach/frequency
- Less targetable than some other media, e.g., magazines, radio, internet
- High clutter & competitive activity
- Declining effectiveness and commercial audiences
- Increased commercial zapping with growth of DVR penetration
- Production and talent costs can be very high

TV Universe

	TV HH (MM)	% Cable	% ADS	% DVR	% HD Capable
2013	116	90	31	87	73
2000	101	69	11	NA	NA
1990	92	56	--	NA	NA
% Ch.	+26	25	+181	+++	NA

Source: Nielsen, TVB

TV Expenditures (Billions)

	Network	Spot	Local	Syndicated	Cable
2013	$14	$21	NA	$2	$24
1990	10	8	8	1	3
% Ch.	+12	+44	NA	+80	+770

Source: LNA, Magna Global, 2020 estimates

TV Reach Potential

Reached Yesterday	Adults	A25-54	HH $75K+
2012	88%	87%	90%
Avg. Hours Spent	4.4	4.1	3.8
2008	90%	90%	94%
Avg. Hours Spent	4.4	4.1	3.8

Source: Nielsen Media Research/TVB,2012

TV Usage Trends

- The following table shows the average percentage of households or persons with TV sets on by month.
- Demonstrates seasonality of primetime viewing by month as well as differences of household vs. TV usage by age group.
- Is television viewing in decline?
- Not according to the data: HUTS/PUTS stable since 2001

Average Prime Time Viewing Levels by Month

Month	Households	A 18-34	A25-54	A55+	HH Index
September	58%	30%	37%	51	99
October	60	32	39	52	103
November	61	32	40	53	103
December	59	31	39	53	101
January	62	32	41	55	101
February	62	33	41	56	105
March	59	30	38	52	103
April	58	29	37	51	101
May	57	29	36	50	98
June	55	27	35	48	94
July	54	26	33	47	91
August	55	28	34	48	94
12-Mo. Avg.	**59**	**30**	**38**	**52**	**100**

Source: Nielsen Media Research

Primetime HUT/PUT Trends

- Television viewing levels have changed little since 2001
- Consistent viewing by age
- PUTS continues to increase with age

HUTS/PUTS by Age

	HH	A18-34	A25-54	A55+
2001	59.1	31.6	39.4	51.1
2003	59.4	30.7	39.1	51.6
2005	60.0	31.1	39.5	51.7
2007	58.9	31.1	38.0	50.5
2009	58.6	30.4	37.9	51.5
2012	60.4	29.7	39.4	53.9

Source: Nielsen Media Research

Television Rating Benchmarks

All Time Highest Rated Programs

Program	HH Rating	Share %
M*A*S*H (Final 2/28/83)	60.2	77
Dallas (11/21/80)	53.3	76
Fugitive (Final 8/27/67)	49.9	72
Gone with the Wind	47.5	70
Bob Hope (1/15/70)	46.6	64
2010 Super Bowl	46.4	68
ABC Theatre (11/23/83)	46.0	62
Roots Mini Series	45.6	varied
Cheers Final (5/20/93)	45.5	64
Ed Sullivan/Beatles	45.3	60
Beverly Hillbillies (1/8/64)	44.0	65.0
Bob Hope 1/14/71)	43.0	61
Academy Awards (4/7/70)	43.4	78
Thorn Birds (3/29/83)	43.2	62
Movie/Airport (11/11/73)	42.3	63

Selected Top Programs, 2011/2012 Season

Program	Network	AA (HH)
Super Bowl	NBC	47.0
NFC Championship	FOX	30.6
AFC Championship	CBS	27.4
AFC Playoff	CBS	22.6
Academy Awards	ABC	22.6
Grammy Awards	CBS	21.7
NFC Playoff	FOX	20.5
AFC Playoff	CBS	`18.5
NFL Playoff	ABC	18.2
Super Bowl Pre Game	NBC	16.9
World Series #7	FOX	15.4
NFL National	NBC	13.8
Oscars	ABC	14.3
BCS Championship	ESPN	14.0
Macy's Thanksgiving Parade	NBC	11.7
Dancing with the Stars	ABC	11.2
American Idol	FOX	11.1
NCIS	CBS	10.8
Rose Bowl	ESPN	10,2
Golden Globes	NBC	10.2
CMA Awards	ABC	9.9

Top Reality Shows

Program	Network	HH Rating
Oscars Red Carpet Live	ABC	15.6
American Idol	FOX	14.5
Dancing with Stars	ABC	13.8
Bachelor After	ABC	9.3
Survivor Nicaragua	CBS	7.9
America's Got Talent	NBC	7.8
Secret Millionaire	ABC	6.6
Voice	FOX	6.6
Survivor South Pacific	CBS	7.3
Mobbed	FOX	6.4

Source: TVB 2012

Top Specials of All Time

Program	Timing	HH Rating
M*A*S*H (last episode)	1983	60.2
Dallas (Who shot JR)	1980	53.3
Roots	1977	51.1
Super Bowl	1982	49.1
Winter Olympics	1994	48.5
Super Bowl XX	1986	48.3
Gone with the Wind Pt I	1976	47.7
Gone With the Wind Pt II	1976	47.4
Bob Hope Christmas Show	1970	46.6
The Day After	1983	46.0

Evening News Ratings

Program	HH Rating	A25-54 Rating
ABC World News	5.0	1.6
CBS Evening News	4.1	1.5
NBC Nightly News	5.5	2.0
Univision	1.0	.7
CNN	.4	.1
Fox News	1.3	.4
HLN	..2	.1
MSNBC	.5	.2

Source: Nielsen, 1st & 2nd Qtrs., 2012

*"The one function that **TV news** performs very well is that when there is no news we give it to you with the same emphasis as if there were"*
---David Brinkley

Television CPM Homes Trends

- The following table shows CPM trends for network and spot television by daypart.
- As forecast i-1020n the 2009 Thumbnail Media Planners, prices as measured by CPM, generally fell in2009/2010 as demand dropped due to budget cutbacks and dipped more in 2011.
- By 2013, primetime prices have recovered to pre-recession levels.
- Network & spot primetime CPMs have increased about 5% per year, while M-F daytime CPMs have increased about 6% per year.
- Advertisers pay a premium for geographic targeting; Spot television CPMs have risen slightly faster than network CPMs

CPM Trends by Daypart

	1990	2000	2004	2007	2008	2009	2013
Network							
Prime	$9.74	$13.42	$19.85	$22.87	$26.22	$22.72	25.06
Index	*100*	*138*	*204*	*235*	*269*	*233*	*257*
M-F Day	2.46	4.35	4.59	6.47	6.53	7.51	6.69
Index	*100*	*177*	*187*	*263*	*265*	*305*	*272*
E. News	5.41	5.89	5.85	7.37	8.17	7.21	7.10
Index	*100*	*109*	*108*	*136*	*151*	*133*	*131*
Late	6.97	9.15	10.87	10.83	11.46	9.45	8.24
Index	*100*	*131*	*156*	*155*	*164*	*136*	*118*
Spot							
Prime	$11.56	$24.55	$27.27	$34.12	$27.67	$30.33	$34.83
Index	*100*	*207*	*234*	*295*	*239*	*262*	*301*
M-F Day	4.07	6.34	5.54	6.66	6.22	7.66	8.72
Index	*100*	*156*	*136*	*164*	*149*	*188*	*114*
E. News	5.73	11.35	10.35	11.35	9.96	11.11	11.15
Index	*100*	*198*	*181*	*198*	*174*	*194*	*195*
Late Eve	6.27	11.53	10.00	12.33	10.35	12.09	12.91
Index	*100*	*184*	*159*	*197*	*165*	*193*	*206*

Source: TVB/Nielsen Media Research, February each year

2013-2014 Television Season

Ratings, Unit Prices & CPP for Select Programs

2013-2014 Primetime Upfront Buys

Examples of prices paid, ratings, and CPP for selected

	Program	Network	HH Rating	Cost/:30 (000)	CPP
1	Sunday Night Football	NBC	8	$594	$74,250
2	Big Bang Theory	CBS	5.2	317	65,192
3	Modern Family	ABC	4.0	282	70,500
4	Simpsons	FOX	3.0	232	74,000
5	The Voice	NBC	8.0	294	37,000
6	New Girl	FOX	4.0	237	59,500
7	Family Guy	FOX	4.5	206	28,592
8	Scandal	CBS	6.0	207	34,500
10	Gray's Anatomy	ABC	2.6	205	45,000
11	Black List	NBC	3.8	201	52,895
12	2 ½ Men	CBS	4.8	184	38,333
13	X Factor	ABC	4.4	179	44,750
14	Millers	CBS	5.6	174	31,070
15	Once... a Time	ABC	4.0	173	43,250
16	2 Broke Girls	CBS	5.2	176	38,460
17	Crazy Ones	CBS	3.8	167	43,950
18	NCIS LA	CBS	4.4	122	13,260
19	Person of Interest	CBS	8.2	136	16.583
20	Castle	ABC	4.1	124	31,000
21	NCIS	CBS	11.8	160	23,516
22	Mom	CBS	4.2	140	33,330
23	Survivor	CBS	4.0	121	30,250

Sources: Unit costs: Ad Age

Ratings: Early performance and 2020 estimates. Ratings subject to change based on actuals.

Selected programs in 2013/2014 seasons using upfront pricing and initial A25-54 ratings. Which were the best/worst buys?

Source; Advertising Age, TVB, 2020 estimates. Costs are averages from six agen

Forecasting Future Ratings

The Formula

- When buying time in broadcast or cable media, the buyer must speculate on the size and characteristics of future advertising audiences.
- Similar to a stock market analyst projecting the future performance of individual stocks.
- The formula for projecting future ratings is:

Rating = Share x HUTS or PUTS

- Rating is the percentage of a universe (e.g., USA households or a demographic group). A 10 household rating means that 10% of the homes were tuned to a program at the average time.
- Share is each program's percentage of the available viewers. If one million households are watching television and 100,000 are watching Program A, then A's share is 10% (100,000/1,000,000).

Steps to Forecasting Future Ratings

1 – Determine the HUTS/PUTS for the day and time period from historical viewing levels (Nielsen Media Research).
2 – Estimate the share of audience you believe a program should get, considering its historical share trends and competitive programs in the time period.
3 – Multiply the estimated share times HUTS/PUTS = Rating
4 – Rating x universe = number of viewers
5 – Viewers x demographic percentages = number of viewers by demographic group

Example
20 % Share X 50% HUTS = 10 Rating X 116 million homes = 11.6 million homes X number of demographic viewers/set = audience reached.

Recent Television Research & News

Nielsen to Include "Twitter Ratings"?

- Nielsen is making another play to properly account for the increasingly elusive TV viewer. Starting during the 2014-15 season, the media company will add mobile viewers into its TV ratings and dynamic digital ratings.

Nielsen Commercial Audience Ratings (C3)

- The broadcast networks are touting huge audience gains for the fall 2013 season including all the DVR and video-on-demand viewing in the week after shows air. While the supplements to live and same-day viewing are certainly a positive, the numbers look different by the measure that advertisers watch. Take a look at NBC's "The Blacklist," which became the first show to ever add more than 6 million viewers in the seven days after an airing. Its audience for its Sept. 30 episode shot up to 17.9 million viewers after a week from 11.4 million on the day it aired.

- But advertisers do not usually go by Live+7, which measures viewers who watched a show up to seven days after it aired. Advertisers care about commercial ratings, or C3, which is the measure of the commercials watched both live and in the three days following. C3 is the primary metric under which most broadcast prime-time is bought and sold.

- **Nielsen began offering commercial ratings (C3) in October 2013. C3 ratings are supposed to better measure how many sets are tuned at the time a commercial airs, including live audience and DVR replays.**

Future of TV & Video

- David Cooperstein, vice president, research director, Forrester Research, Inc. discussed the results of the latest ANA/Forrester survey on TV and video.
- Key takeaways from the survey: Post-recession, advertisers have a positive view on TV and everything video.

Beyond CPMs and CPP to Ad Exposure

- We strongly support Nielsen's efforts to measure commercial audience. The whole point is to expose consumers to a commercial, not just a program. However, the question of commercial exposure goes beyond audience fall off during breaks or DVR playbacks and commercial zapping.
- Many other factors affect whether consumers will be exposed to a commercial: viewer attention levels, viewer involvement, commercial positioning in a pod, presence of competitive commercials, and so on.
- Some planners use attention levels from syndicated research to adjust audience forecasts and compare audience delivery on an attention adjusted basis. SMRB's attention measures suggest wide variation in viewer attention by daypart, program type and by individual program. For example:

	% Fully Attentive
NBC Today Show	13%
Young & Restless	54
CBS Evening News	37
CBS Survivor	67
CSI	71
CBS 60 Minutes	43

Set Top Box Data (STB)

- There is an initiative underway, involving several industry groups to harness television set top data in order to provide more detailed and accurate audience information.
- As television has become digital and viewing scatters to devices ranging from computer screens to cell phones, old forms of measurement have had difficulty keeping up. Data from the millions of set-top boxes promises to provide more accurate and granular information about TV viewing.
- Most agree that much work still needs to be done before STB data could be considered a viable alternative to the current TV ratings system.

- Several companies are either investigating STB data products, or are already providing data to clients, including Rentrak, Kantar, TNS, TIVO, and Nielsen.
- Proponents of STB data like the large sample sizes—which Are significantly larger than current national and local samples —and could provide accurate data for smaller geographic areas as well as purchasing and demographic groups.

Out of Home TV Viewing

- Arbitron Television (ARB) is using their Portable People Meter (PPM) system to measure out of home viewing in restaurants and bars.
- Of interest to media buyers and sellers alike is that the workplace, airports, and viewing in other peoples/ homes, will increase the size of the measured TV audience.

Network TV

Availabilities

- Major over the air networks: ABC, CBS, NBC, Fox, CW, MNT (formerly WB and UPN), Univision (Spanish), Telemundo (Spanish)
- Plus syndicated networks
- :30 commercial – basic unit of sale/longer and shorter spots available
- All dayparts (early AM, daytime, early evening, primetime, etc.)
- Programming which targets diverse target groups

<u>2014 Super Bowl XLVII</u>
2013 Rating – 46.3/69% Share
Cost/:30: $3.5+ million (CBS)
2014 Cost/:30: $4 million (FOX)

Network TV Coverage vs. Reach

Network Coverage

- Major networks reach majority of households weekly

Network	Language	# Affiliates	HH Coverage	Weekly HH Reach
ABC	English	226	97%	71%
CBS	English	215	97	75
NBC	English	229	97	72
Fox	English	223	96	70
CW	English	204	94	41
MNT	English	162	89	32
Univision	Spanish	46	50	NA
Telemundo	Spanish	46	45	NA

Broadcast TV vs. Cable Daily Reach

- Ad supported cable has higher share of audience than broadcast

	HH Rating	Share
Broadcast Networks	26.9	38.5%
Independents	1.0	1.4
Ad Supported Cable	35.1	50.3
Public	1.2	1.8
Pay Cable	3.0	4.4

Source: Nielsen/TVB

Commercial Mix (TVB)

- Use of short form commercials growing as costs increase
- :30 still basic unit of sale

	:10s/:15s	:30s	:60s+
2000	33%	59%	8%
2009	40	51	9

Source: TVB

2014 Network TV Market Outlook

- Television and network spending remains strong in the 2013-2014 outlook, and up slightly vs. 2012
- Many have been predicting the demise of television advertising, but Mark Twain had it right: "The rumors of my death have been greatly exaggerated."
- Total television spending is projected to increase by 5% to $64 billion in 2014
- Depending on the network, the 2013-2014 upfront market yielded 5-7% CPM increases in primetime, a leading indicator of pricing
- We expect lower average CPM increases for the total year
- Demand for TV and network TV will be driven by the quarterly economies and economic outlooks in 2014; Obamacare will have an impact on spending & budgets.
- 2020's CPP estimates for 2014 assumes a 1.5% average CPP increase (across all dayparts) vs. 2013. Following is our crystal ball

2014 Network TV Cost Estimates (:30 HH CPP)

Daypart	2nd/4th Qtrs	1st/3rd Qtrs	Avg. A25-54
Prime	$24,600	$15,700	$39,900
Early News	11,300	10,000	23,450
Late Night	19,700	16,900	30,300
M-F Daytime	7,050	6450	11,800
Synd. Prime	20,200	18,800	31,200

Source: 2020 Estimates

Table Reads: The prime time cost per HH rating point in the 2nd or 4th quarter (average) is projected at $22,500 for 2012.

Spot Television

Availabilities

- Can buy spots on local TV stations in 210 DMAs
- Over 1300 network affiliates, independent stations, as well as local cable systems
- Programming may be network, locally produced or syndicated
- Spots may run between programs rather than in program

Commercial Mix (TVB)

	:10s/:15s	:30s	:60s+
2000	13%	81%	6%
2008	24	68	8

Spot Television Dayparts

Daypart	Time	Typical Programming
Early AM	6-9A	Kids, info
Morning	9A-12P	News, talk, court
Afternoon	12P-4P	Soaps, game shows
Early fringe	4P-6P	Game shows, news
Early news	6P-7P	Local & network news
Prime access	7P-8P	SitComs, game shows
Prime time	8-11P	Entertainment
Late News	11-11:30P	Local News
Late Fringe	11:30P- 1A	Talk, Comedy, Syndication

2014 Market Outlook

- Thanks to the Olympics and the elections, 2012 was a great year for television, especially local television. 2012 provided networks and a great many TV stations (especially those in "battleground" states), a nice piece of the estimated $3.2 billion political ad spend.

- In 2013, without the Olympics or elections, budgets for spot television were primarily driven by local market economic performance and forecasts for the future.

- Without an improved local economy, or at least a more favorable outlook, national advertisers and retailers probably won't be increasing their spending in local spot TV

- In 2014, 2020 projects an average 1% decrease in spot TV CPPs but this will vary widely by market with local economic and business conditions including Obamacare impacts.

2014 Cost Projections (Cume :30 A25-54 TRPS)

- Use the following data to forecast cost of a spot TV schedule.
- Calculate the cost per 1% of U.S. and project it out to the percentage of households/sales you want to reach.

Cost per Point Based on (Households)

DMA Coverage	% US TV HH	Prime	Early News	Late	M-F Day
Top 10	32.8	$22,700	$9,950	$10,050	$6,600
Top 20	46.9	32,000	13,900	13,000	8,485
Top 30	56.4	33,000	16,200	15,700	10.100
Top 40	63.5	36,000	17,600	17,240	11,100
Top 50	69.3	37,400	18,900	20,000	12,940
Top 60	74.2	39,000	20,300	21,500	13,750
Top 70	78.0	40,790	20,700	21,900	13.550
Top 80	81.4	43,250	22,400	22,250	14,350
Top 90	84.3	45,900	22,800	22,350	14,375
Top 100	87.1	47,300	23,000	22,500	14,550

Source: Industry sources and 2020 estimates

> **Test**: What would it cost to buy 1000 TRPS in primetime in each of the top 100 markets?

Cost per :30 Spot

- Media buying decisions should be made on the basis of cost in relationship to audience and effectiveness (e.g., cost per TRP) rather than cost per spot.)
- For those who need cost per spot, the actual cost per: 30 spot will vary by market, day part, station, program, timing, and supply & demand conditions.
- For example in the top 10 markets the cost per spot in the top 10 markets would approximate the following based on Nielsen ratings and our cost estimates:

Top 10 DMAs	Avg. HH Rating	HH CPP	Cost/:30
Prime	5.0	$22,700	$113,500
Daytime	2.0	6,600	13,200
Early news	4.0	9,950	39,800
Late Night	4.0	10,050	40,200

Cable Television

Availabilities

- 80+ ad supported cable networks
- 10,000+ individual cable systems
- Local cable interconnects (networks of local cable systems)
- Local cable systems to cover communities
- Network reruns & increasingly **original programming**

Ad Supported Cable Overview

Cable Audience Situation	2012
Total Cable TV Household Penetration	90%
Ad Supported Network Penetration	77
Share of HH Viewing – total day	45
Share of HH Viewing – prime time	48
Weekly TV HH Reach	82%

Source: TVB, CAB

Broadcast vs. Cable TV Reach Potential

- Cable TV can deliver high reach and could be considered as an alternative to broadcast
- Given cable's cost efficiency advantage vs. broadcast, a heavy cable plan may provide reach comparable to bdcst.

Network	Cume Weekly Reach (HH)
ABC/CBS/NBC	94%
All Cable Channels	84
ESPN	35
TBS	34
USA	33
FX	32
TNT	30
HIST	29
AEN	27
AMC	25

Source: Nielsen, TVB, 2020 estimates

Broadcast vs. Cable Cumes

- MYTH: Cable reach is too limited to use without broadcast
- TRUTH: Can achieve comparable reach in broadcast or cable.

Target	Broadcast Cume	Cable Cume
Adults 18-34	54%	58%
Adults 18-49	60	64
Adults 25-54	85	68
Teens 12-17	43	62
Children 6-11	36	63

Source: TVB, CAB, 2020 estimates

Al Jazeera America Update

- Now available in 55 million homes (incl. Time Warner)
- Major expansion planned, people & programming
- Poor ratings to date, e.g., average <20,000 average viewers vs. 1MM+ on Fox News

Cable Network
Audience Composition

Network	Description	% Men	% Women	18-34	25-54	35-64	Med Inc
A&E	Movies, Drama, Bibliog.	47	53	36	57	60	$60
BET	Black Ent't	48	52	53	57	41	46
BRAVO	Entertainment	40	60	32	60	55	59
CNBC	Business/Finance	54	46	24	56	49	73
CNN	24 Hour News	51	49	22	53	56	69
COMEDY	Original comedy	59	41	46	62	49	69
DISNEY	Family	37	63	41	63	38	60
ESPN	Sports	72	28	32	57	53	73
FOOD NET	Food/Cook/Lifestyle	36	64	30	59	59	69
FOX BIZ	Business/Finance	80	20	32	58	52	78
FNC	Fox News Channel	51	49	20	53	58	68
FX	Movies, Original Pg.	56	44	44	63	50	67
GOLF CH.	Live Golf, Instruction	77	23	19	46	54	87
HALLMRK	Movies/Specials	33	67	14	45	59	53
HISTORY	History	62	38	28	56	57	69
HGTV	Home & Garden TV	35	65	23	63	64	78
HLN	Headline News	55	45	15	58	64	69
HSN	Home Shopping Net.	27	73	20	54	62	70
LIF	Lifetime/Women's	27	73	27	56	57	56
MSNBC	News & Talk	52	48	23	58	60	72
MTV	Music/Pop Culture	49	51	66	59	33	61
NAT GEO	Exploration/Culture	59	41	26	58	58	70
NICK NITE	Comedy/Family	39	61	44	71	50	56
NICHELOD	Children's Programs	42	58	45	66	50	61
OXYGEN	Personalities	26	74	34	61	56	59
QVC	Shopping Network	23	77	13	47	63	61
SPEED	Motor Sports	78	22	33	62	58	51
SPIKE TV	Male Programs	70	30	43	62	51	62
SYFY	Science Fiction	60	40	30	62	45	61
TBS	Gen. Ent. /Movies	51	49	37	62	53	67
TNT	Drama/Entertain	52	48	31	58	55	65
USA	Orig.Movies/Drama	51	49	33	59	55	65

Source: CAB

Recent Cable TV Research
How People Use Television

- SRI/Knowledge Network study conducted for CAB found that "television is television." There is no inherent effectiveness advantage for broadcast television in terms of recall and other traditional measures. Hence: the **One TV World** moniker.

- Study found that viewers search for what to watch without regard to origin, whether a broadcast or cable outlet.
- Many cable channels have loyal viewers, just like TV networks or channels do.
- Cable channels can achieve high reach—even without the inclusion of broadcast.
- Is broadcast more effective than cable? Studies of viewer attention to programs find that cable is as effective as broadcast and other studies find no correlation between rating size and commercial recall.

Source:2020 estimates, CAB, various studies

Unaided Recall Study

- Nielsen conducted a study of commercial recall in cable vs. broadcast programming
- No difference in recall was found
- Channel surfing during breaks is comparable
- Commercial recall is affected by length of commercial pod and position within the pod (as was found with broadcast).

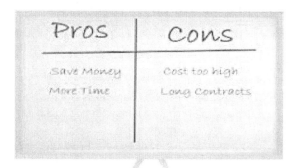

Cable TV Market Outlook

- Continuing previous trends, ad revenues in cable television have surpassed revenues in broadcast network TV by a wide margin.

- Cable revenues are forecast at $26+ billion vs. $13 billion on the traditional broadcast networks, and it is expected that cable will receive an increased share of national broadcast spending.
- Cable is increasing its share of the TV market vs. broadcast television for a variety of reasons including the following.
- In times of increased concerns about cost efficiency and getting the most "bang for the buck," cable continues its lead.
- Cable targets many narrowcast audiences that broadcast TV can't: cooking, nature, finance, news and politics, and so on.
- In order to attract larger, quality audiences, cable programming has improved dramatically, including a lot of original programming.
- Cable is at the forefront of new addressability targeting methodologies, while broadcast is stuck with their old low tech distribution model.
- We estimate an average 5% increase in cable TV prices as the industry attempts to close the gap with broadcast network pricing.

2014 Cable TV :30 Cost Projections

- The cost of commercial spots on cable TV vary widely, from as little as $2,000 or less to nearly $1 million for a major special/sports event
- In general, cable spots will cost $3000-$5000 + and $10,000+ on premium channels; spots on the higher rated TNT and ESPN channels may cost up to $27,000 per :30, depending on audience size.
- It is a mistake to measure cable TV ad costs by the cost per spot rather than the cost per point (CPP) paid based on the total market. (Beware: cable networks often report ratings based on their coverage areas rather than total US-- which means that a spot with a 1 rating in 50% of the country really has a .5 total US rating).
- Following are 2020's projections of primetime cable cost per points on the larger networks/channels.

Estimated 2013 Prime Time :30 CPP – Major Nets

	2nd 4th Qtrs	1st/3rd Qtrs
HH CPP	$25,200	$22,500
A25-54 CPP	38,000	34,000

> *Cable TV prices are closing the gap*
> *with broadcast television prices (CPP)*

3

Radio

Radio Outlook in 2014

A synthesized planning guide for network and spot radio for 2014. Data on audiences, costs, & research are included along with our exclusive 2014 market forecast and projected costs

Radio

Advantages

- Demographic targeting by radio format
- Engagement with loyal station audiences
- Build high frequency with a station's audience
- Lower CPMs and out of pocket costs
- Reach impulse buyers out of home
- Station's on air talent, promotion & merchandising opportunities

Disadvantages

- Audience fragmentation – over 10,000 stations dividing up the available listening audience.
- Satellite radio further fragmenting a small audience.
- Results in very small ratings for most stations.
- Acquiring significant reach may require use of many stations.
- Low attention levels, especially for music formats (higher for news/talk and sports).
- Lack of visuals restricts communication and use of sensory appeals.
- Smaller coverage areas vs. television, requires more stations to cover a DMA.
- Radio's daily reach appears to be declining (see chart below)
- Radio requires its audience to visualize (theatre of the mind). *"It's not true I had nothing on. I had the radio on!*

Radio Expenditures

	Network	National Spot	Local Spot
2013E	1.2	NA	14.8
1992	.4	1.5	6.9
% Ch.	+200	NA	+114

Source: RAB/CM

It's not true that I had nothing on. I had the radio on.
–Marilyn Monroe

"Reached Yesterday" by Radio

- In 2012, Nielsen reported a lower percentage of people listening to radio "yesterday."

Year	Adults	Adults 25-54	HH$ 50+
2008	73%	82%	81%
2012	59	66	63

Source: Nielsen, TVB

Radio Effectiveness

- Among national advertisers, the cost effectiveness of radio advertising has long been a concern.
- Visit RAB.com for a variety of recent case studies on how radio was used effectively for a broad spectrum of advertisers.

Radio Market Outlook

- Forecasts of radio volume in 2014 again varies from no growth to 1+% growth depending on the market.

- Since 80% of radio spending is local, the radio business in 2014 will be driven by anticipated improved consumer confidence (varies by market) and changes in retail sales, and automotive sales in particular.

- Local Radio will benefit from continued strong auto dealer sales.

- For many national advertisers, the concern continues as to how cost effective radio is due to low listener attention levels and huge commercial clutter.

- The Nielsen study cited earlier also found that a declining percentage of people are listening to radio.

- 2014 Forecast: On balance, we project 0-1 or 2% CPP increase for radio.

Audience Composition by Format

- According to Arbitron, different radio station formats reach different target audiences.
- Table reads; 42.2% of news/talk station listeners are 65+ years old.
- Examples of age demographics by station format:

Format	P12+	M 25-54	W25-54	P65+
A/C	14.0	10.3	21.2	10.9
Alternative	3.4	4.6	3.2	0.3
CHR	10.9	7.2	10.7	0.9
Classical	1.0	0.5	0.6	3.3
Country	9.7	8.2	10.5	11.3
Adult Standards	1.0	0.3	0.3	4.8
Smooth Jazz	2.8	2.3	2.7	4.6
News/Talk	17.4	20.1	8.2	42.2
Oldies	5.5	5.6	5.6	4.7
Religious	2.7	1.8	3.7	3.9
Rock	7.9	14.4	5.9	0.8
Spanish	11.0	12.5	12.0	6.9
Urban	9.8	8.4	12.1	4.1

> **Why do some media planners say radio's advantage is *"Theatre of the Mind?"***

Where Listening Occurs

Daypart	Home	Car	Work	Other
Mon-Sun 6-10 AM	39%	35%	23%	3%
M-F 6-10 AM	38	38	23	1
M-F 10A – 3PM	29	30	39	2
M-F 3-7PM	31	45	22	2
M-F 7P - Midnight	58	28	10	4
Weekend	48	38	10	4

Sources: RAB and Arbitron

Network Radio

Availabilities

- Approximately 55 national radio networks are measured by Arbitron
- Each network has a format, e.g., Adult Contemporary
- :60 or :30 commercials are available

Source: Arbitron, 9/12

Radio Networks Measured by RADAR

- Networks come and go with regularity
- 65 networks measured by RADAR
- Network Groups

Groups	Number Networks
American Urban	4
Chrystal	4
Cumulus	9
Premiere	15
United	1
Westwood One	14

Source: Arbitron

Weekly Reach Potential of Radio Networks

	Adults 18+	Ad 18-49	Ad 25-54
All Networks	71%	72%	72%

2014 Network Radio Cost Estimates (:60s)

- Network radio CPPs/CPMs will vary widely, depending on networks selected, audiences, timing
- :30s are normally the unit of sale; shown here are :60s to make cost comparisons to spot

Network Radio Cost Example

Coverage	Comm'l Length**	CPP Adults
National	:60	$4050

*Caution: actual coverage may range from under 50% to over 90%, depending on the network and its affiliates at a point in time **Assumes a daypart mix

Spot Radio

Availabilities

- 10,000+ stations/about 50 per average DMA
- Basic unit of sale is a :60 commercial, although :30s may be purchased, often at 80% of the minute rate
- Day parts Sold: morning and afternoon drive time, daytime, night, weekend
- Sponsorships often available of program or sports events
- Station merchandising and promotion & use of good on air talent available

Common Dayparts

- Day parts relate to the time of day listening occurs-- which vary in audience size and demographics
- Buy time during desired day parts on desired stations
- Day parts vary in audience size and demographics
- For example, night time listening skews heavily toward teens and young adults while the daytime audience, not surprisingly, is women.

Daypart	Description	Target
M-F 6A-10A	Morning Drive	Any
M-F 10A-3P	Daytime	Women
3-7	PM Drive	Any
6A-7P	ROS	Any
7P - Mid	Evening	P12-34
Sa/Sun 10A-7P	Weekend	Shoppers

Popular Radio Formats

- Radio stations attract mass or highly targeted audiences with their programming formats.
- The following table provides a summary of how radio formats attract different demographic audiences:

Format	Target	Share of Audience (12+)
Adult Contemporary	Women	13

Contemporary Hit	Young Women	1
News/Talk/Sports	P45+, men	7
Country	Slightly female	9
Oldies	P12+	6
AOR	Men 18-34	4
Classic Rock	Men 35-54	11
Alternative	Slightly male	3
Adult Standards	P65+	3
Spanish	Hispanics	8
Urban	Teens, 18-24	10
Religious	Psychographic	3

Radio Audience Measurement: (PPM)

- Accurate measurement of radio audiences has long been a problem or an issue to buyers
  Arbitron has now rolled out its **Portable People Meters (PPMs)** to the top US markets, while diaries continue to be used in smaller markets.
- Personal People Meters are devices carried by people in Arbitron's samples which automatically record and report to Arbitron computers what radio the respondent has on (does not record commercial exposure or response).
- PPMs will be a good business develop tool for radio as they will be able to better measure true audiences, which are higher than those measured by the diary system.

2014 Spot Radio Cost Estimates (:60 CPP)

- Use the following data to quickly cost out a schedule in the top 10-200 metro markets by multiplying the CPP times the desired number of TRPS (adults, men, women)
- If your goal is to support a given percentage of the population, e.g., 15%, calculate the cost of reaching 1% in the appropriate market group and multiply it times the desired coverage percentage.
- 20014 CPP estimates assume 0% increase vs. 2013
  Assumes average 1.5% price increase in 2013; actuals will vary

Metros	% US HH	CPP A25-54	CPP M25-54	CPP W25-54
Top 10	26	4670	4460	5000
Top 20	35	6700	5550	6200
Top 30	42	8080	7150	8550
Top 40	47	8700	9000	10100
Top 50	50	10500	9950	10950
Top 60	54	11250	10750	11900
Top 70	56	11800	11050	12400
Top 80	59	12500	11560	13000
Top 90	60	12850	12100	13860
Top 100	62	13250	12400	14000
Top 150	69	14000	14459	16200
Top 200	72	15000	15350	17700

Note: Based on day part mix

Would you rather have 1000 TRPS in radio or 400 TRPS in television?

4
Magazines

A Quick Consumer Magazine Reference

A quick consumer magazine reference including reach potential, magazine research, 2014 market outlook and cost estimates for 75 magazines.

Magazines

Availabilities

- 17,000 magazines = a magazine for every interest
- Ad Units Available – fractional and full pages, spreads, cover gatefolds, preprinted inserts, advertorials, etc.
- Coloration: B/W, 4C, 2C, 3C, 5C, matched colors
- Positioning: inside page, 2nd, 3rd or back cover, opposite relevant editorial or Run of Book
- Special editorial sections and tie ins
- Geographic Editions – national, regions of US, individual markets, test market editions (some magazines
- Some demographic editions, e.g., high income, students, military
- Still weak in digital editions, but growing

Advantages

- Choice of broad or selective reach
- Target special interest audiences & psychographics
- Creative flexibility
- Geographic flexibility
- Potential for relevant context
- Great for considered purchase products and products requiring more explanation & information
- Appetite appeal
- Coupon and promotional opportunities
- Reach lighter TV viewers
- Add synergies to media mix communication
- Placing URL in ad increases website visits

Disadvantages

- Selective perception; not intrusive; easy to skip ads
- Builds reach more slowly than broadcast media
- Lack of immediacy/Not intrusive
- Long lead times for closing

Reach Potential

- According to Nielsen, in 2012, the percentage of every demographic group "reached by magazines yesterday" decreased by about 50% vs. 2008 so it may be getting more difficult to reach many targets via magazines.

Reached Yesterday	% Adults	% A25-54	% HH $50+K
2008	50	48	56
2010	29	28	41
2012	**25**	**20**	**28**

Source: Nielsen, TVB, 2008-2010, 2012

Magazine Recall by Type of Ad

Type of Ad	Recall Index
Full page	100
Inside Front Cover	112
Back Cover	100
Multi Page Units	115
Two Page Spread	117
Less than Full Page (Fractional Page)	81
Four Color	110
Spot Color	102
Black and White	87
First Half of Magazine	100
Second Half of Magazine	98

New Magazine Research

The magazine industry continues to sponsor research which will persuade advertisers to include magazines in their media mix, e.g., along with television and online advertising. Following are two examples.   Should you use magazines?

"Great hitting beats great pitching and vice versa."
--Casey Stengel, Former Yankees Manager

Assessing Ad Impact

The Magazine Publishers Association has published a compilation and analysis of 39 cross media studies by Dynamic Logic and Cross Media Research, companies which specializes Assessing Ad Impact: How TV, Online and Magazines Contribute Throughout the Purchase Funnel.

Not surprisingly, the analysis concludes that magazines in combination with television were more effective in driving more favorable attitudes and behavior than television alone or television in combination with online.

Marketing Mix Modeling & Media Inputs

Advertisers use marketing mix models to guide media investments and predict future results. The MPA worked with a variety of outside media and research organizations to develop more precise media inputs –such as magazine audience accumulation data—to best predict marketing results.

2014 Magazine Market Outlook

- Business is bad. Profits are bad.
- 2014 could be a year of opportunity for magazine advertisers who are able and willing to negotiate deeper off card deals to achieve lower prices.
- While 2011-13 were expected to begin a rebound for magazine advertising, but ad budget cuts resulted in a 2.8% reduction in ad pages.
- Perhaps most damaging is that increased digital spending is being funded out of magazine budget cuts.
- Caution: A large percentage of magazines included in this analysis have cut circulation while raising rates.
- The future of magazines is digital In 2012, only 6.6% of revenues were digital, while 41% was print and 53% was print advertising. Veronis Suhler forecasts that by 2016, revenues will be 15% digital, 37% print circulation, and 48% print advertising.

Leading Magazines by Category
Total Audience & Costs (000)
CPM Circulation

MAGAZINE	Circ.	Cost P4C	Total Adults	Med. Age	HH Income
Automotive					
Car & Driver	1318	$187	10841	37.4	$75.7
Hot Rod	663	92	6554	39.1	55.2
Motor Trend	1096	165	7607	38.8	71.4
Road & Track	709	153	5338	41.8	82.8
Business/Money					
Entrepreneur	617	84	2238	41.9	78.9
Forbes	914	122	5499	44.7	95.0
Fortune	851	125	4017	43.4	99.2
Inc.	711	76	1465	41.7	87.8
Kiplinger's	817	54	2363	55.1	102.9
Money	1918	202	7650	48.1	92.5
Wall Street Jrnl	1673	224	3395	50.1	138.0
Computer					
PC World	541	NA	3962	39.7	77.3
Entertainment					
People	3450	214	44707	40.9	69.1
TV Guide	2000	154	18002	44.8	47.8
Ethnic Interest					
Black Enterprise	528	42	3890	41.5	51.8
Ebony	1302	61	7836	40.7	43.5
Jet	887	30	7543	42.0	41.5
Latina	507	42	2831	35.3	41.6
Family/Parenting					
American Baby	1986	194	6697	30.2	48.8
Parenting	2203		9393	33.7	57.5
Parents	2205	168	15379	33.9	61.5
Scholast. Parent.	1375	105	7785	34.6	51.8
Food					
Bon Appétit	1353	144	6502	48.9	91.2
Cooking Light	1772	115	11397	48.3	80.8

Magazine					
Food & Wine	999	87	7776	44.5	83.1
General Interest					
Nat'l Geographic	4100	225	31649	46.7	69.2
Readers Digest	5500	185	30527	52.9	61.2
Smithsonian	2025	136	6851	53.0	64.9
Health					
Prevention	3313	135	10340	53.9	64.9
Men's Health	1860	178	11876	38.3	82.3
Weight Watchers	1294	74	10488	44.7	64.0
Home					
BH & G	7600	507	4934	48.9	66.1
Country Living	1620	59	11198	51.2	60.4
House Beautiful	823	121	6242	53.3	71.1
Mature					
AARP the Mag.	24556	533	35230	62.1	57.9
Men's					
Maxim	2537	254	12805	29.7	69.5
Playboy	1500	113	8436	35.4	59.0
Popular Mech.	1207	130	8791	45.3	70.0
Popular Science	1320	124	7129	43.8	74.3
News					
Time	3250	320	20172	47.3	75.6
Newsweek	LAST PRINT EDITION 12/12				
US News & WR	1366	90	11208	50.8	76.3
Regional					
Midwest Living	959	129	4050	52.2	69.8
Southern Living	2840	179	16034	51.2	72.6
Sunset	1224	108	4925	51.9	73.6
Sports					
ESPN the Mag.	2059	216	14702	32.4	67.4
Field & Stream	1514	116	9115	45.9	58.7
Golf Digest	1678	123	6008	48.8	94.9
Golf Magazine	1427	175	5577	48.2	92.5
Outdoor Life	818	67	5641	45.5	57.4
Sports Illustrated	3150	392	21012	39.3	72.8
Travel					
Frommer's	695		2431	48.4	77.0
CondeNast Travl	821	119	3429	49.1	105.8
Nat'l Geo Travelr	699	73	7519	42.2	70.0
Travel & Leisure	958	112	4877	49.1	97.5
Cosmopolitan	2907	222	18401	31.2	61.5

Family Circle	3833	255	19591	51.6	58.7
Glamour	2390	201	12310	34.7	68.3
Good Housekeep	4630	345	24205	51.6	61.0
Martha Stewart	2031	158	10976	48.2	74.3
O, Oprah Mag.	2398	151	15338	45.9	72.8
Redbook	2223	153	8466	47.5	68.5
Woman's Day	3934	260	20633	50.6	58.1

Source: MRI-Plus, 2012

Is this the future of magazines?

5

Newspapers

A Quick Guide to Newspapers

*A reference for newspapers, traditionally the #1 local
advertising medium. This section includes an overview, audience
and readership data as well as cost benchmarks.*

Newspapers

Availabilities

- National newspapers (e.g., Wall Street Journal, USA Today)
- Dailies & Sunday editions
- Weeklies & suburban papers
- Free/rack distributed
- Sections of newspapers: main news, sports, business, home, life, special sections
- Creative units: Full and fractional pages in one inch increments, free standing inserts, polybags
- Geographic Flexibility: full run vs. geographic zones
- Color: Most newspapers now offer quality four color

Advantages

- News environment provides sense of immediacy for retailers
- Immediate distribution and readership for announcements/news
- Local market and zone flexibility
- Consumers shop ads to identify who offers the best deals
- Can often target zip codes with free standing inserts & samples
- Short closing dates – can get ad in paper quickly

Disadvantages

- High out of pocket cost and high CPMs
- 100%+ premium for national advertisers
- Broad, older audience; not as targetable as many other media
- Declining circulation
- High advertising clutter makes it difficult to be seen
- High logistics: differing mechanical requirements; complex rate cards, rigid policies, etc.
- Heavy cost cutting may lead to lower product quality and a self-fulfilling prophesy for the future

Market Outlook 2014

- The newspaper industry has already lost over 60% of its revenues since 2008, and there is no end in sight.
- The outlook for newspapers worsens as newspapers reduce their value and readers go to free broadcast and online news sources --and retail coupons and offers.
- Newspapers now appear to be stabilizing a little. Some newspapers are trying to develop new income streams.
- Advertising spending outlook for 2014 is again bleak from the newspapers' point of view. As shown below, circulation continues to decline even for the most important papers in the country, an average of 32% vs. 2009 for the newspapers included in this panel. Nielsen's study reported here also finds that a rapidly declining percentage of adults are reading newspapers. Yet, the majority of newspapers are simultaneously increasing rates
- NET: Newspapers need revenue: negotiate better rates!

Print Circulation Trends – Newspapers (000)

Newspaper	2009 Circulation	2013 Circulation
New York Times	1,000.0	731.2
NY Daily News	633.0	360.5
NY Post	625.0	300.0
LA Times	739.0	432.9
Chicago Tribune	516.0	368.2
Chicago Sun Times	313.0	184.8
Philadelphia Inquirer	441.0	184.8
San Francisco Chronicle	339.9	220.0
Boston Globe	324.0	149.5
Dallas Morning News	339.0	190.6
Washington Post	623.0	431.1
Atlanta Journal/Const.	275.0	162.0
Total	**6167.0**	**3715.6**

Newspaper Reach Potential

- Nielsen data reports substantiate large decreases in newspaper readership, 2012 vs. 2008, in all demographic groups
- Highest incidence of readership among higher income adults
- Does not include digital readers

Read Yesterday	% Adults	% A25-54	% HH $75K+
2008	64%	56%	69%
2010	39	33	38
2012	36	27	35

Source: Nielsen surveys, TVB, 2008-20012

Section Readership

- Readership varies by section of newspaper by target audience
- Which section delivers the largest audiences among all demos?

	News	Bus.	Ent't	Sports	Food	Class
Adults	90%	62%	68%	61%	57%	55%
Men	89	67	62	76	49	57
Women	91	66	74	48	66	53

National Newspapers (Print & Digital)

- WSJ leads in print and total circulation
- NYT leads in digital circulation
- USA Today third in total circulation

Newspaper	Print Circ. (000)	Digital Circ. (000)	Total (000)
USA Today	1424	250	1674
Wall Street Journal	1481	898	2379
NY Times	731	1134	1865

Newspaper Distributed Magazines (2013)

	Est. Circ. (000)	Est.CostP4C $(000)	CPM
USA Weekend	22,250	$693.1	$31.15
Parade	33,000	1071.1	33.55
NY Times Magazine	1,645	107.1	65.05
WSJ Weekend (US)	1,600	151.1	94.43

*Latest available

USSPI (Suburban Press) – Latest Available Data

- Suburban newspapers generally exclude the core city area
- May be used to target suburban areas rather than whole market
- Audiences tend to be higher income, better educated
- Issue is often whether they are read as thoroughly as a good daily newspaper
- May be ordered as a network buy through USSPI who will issue insertion orders and distribute print materials

# DMAs	60+
Total Circulation	14.5 million
Cost P B/W	$1,395,000
CPM	$96.25

Free Standing Inserts

Newspapers routinely distribute insert free-standing inserts to full circulation area, zone, or zips containing the desired target households

- Select zip codes where insert to be dropped
- Inserts may be supplied or printed by the newspaper

Cost of Free Standing Insert	CPM
Insertion in Newspapers (8 P)	$50+
Printing (BIG Variable) (4c)	$500-1500+
Shipping & Misc.	20
Total	$1500++

- In addition, advertisers may participate in an insert supplied by Valassis, Carol Wright, or another insert printer/distributor. These firms print and distribute advertisers' inserts in newspapers on a turnkey basis.

Daily Newspapers - Estimated 2013 Costs

- Current costs difficult to determine because many publishers have not submitted their rate cards/circulation statistics to SRDS
- Digital circulation growing
- Based on recent data, it would cost over $2 million to run a ¼ page newspaper ad in the top 100 DMAs (87% of US), assuming a Sunday insertion.
- Weekday circulation and costs are lower
- Determining ad size and weekday vs. Sunday decisions are important to accurate cost and audience delivery estimates

DMAs	% US HH	Cost ¼P B/W Sunday (000)
Top 10	32.8	$709
Top 20	46.9	1070
Top 30	56.4	1310
Top 40	63.5	1420
Top 50	69.3	1530
Top 60	74.2	1650
Top 70	78.0	1785
Top 80	81.4	1950
Top 90	84.3	2100
Top 100	87.1	2275

Table Reads:

It would cost approximately $709,000 to run a quarter Page B/W ad in major Sunday newspapers (print editions only) in the top 10 DMAs covering about 33% of US households

Selected Daily Newspapers
National Ad Rates (2012)

**Latest available rates, does not include digital.**
**Table Reads**: A 1000 column inch ad in the New York Times would cost $119,600, based on the national open rate (1000 inches x $1196 per inch = $119,600).

Market/ Newspaper	Households (000)	M/E	Daily Circulation	Open Cost/Inch
New York	6962			
NY Times		M	720	$1196
NY Daily News		M	429	883
NY Post		M	408	873
Newsday		M	315	770
Los Angeles	4412			
LA Times		M	516	972
Orange Co. Register		M	159	362
Chicago	3540			
Tribune		M	404	755
Sun Times		M	214	632
Philadelphia	2236			
Inquirer		**M**	**261**	**615**
San Francisco	1611			
SF Chronicle		A	220	613
Oakland Tribune		M	93	252
SF Examiner		M	106	33
Boston	1732			
Globe		M	194	577
Herald		M	106	386
Dallas/FW	2390			
Dallas Morning News		M	209	650
Fort Worth Star/Tel		M	154	429
Washington DC	2113			

Washington Post		M	475	856
Washington Times		M	67	108
Miami/FL	**2157**			
Herald		M	120	283
Atlanta	**2070**			
Journal Constitution		M	162	566
Detroit	**1717**			
News/Free Press		M	216	727
Houston	**2134**			
Chronicle		M	255	676
Seattle	**1371**			
Times/Post Intell.		M	252	539
Tacoma Tribune		M	222	102
Minneapolis/SP	**1280**			
Minn. Tribune		M	239	318
SP Pioneer Press		M	135	232
Tampa/St. Pete	**1178**			
Tampa Tribune		M	216	770
St. Pete Times		M	145	435
Cleveland	**832**			
Plain Dealer		M	229	520
Phoenix	**1619**			
Arizona Republic		M	288	495
Riverside/SB	**1387**			
Press Ent.		ME	93	NA
St. Louis	**1119**			
Post Dispatch		M	167	NA
San Diego	**1065**			
Union Tribune		M	202	459
Baltimore	**1047**			
Sun		M	171	328
Pittsburgh	**971**			
Post Gazette		M	173	303

Denver	**1000**			
Post		M	297	862
Portland, O	**887**			
Oregonian		A	204	255
Cincinnati	**835**			
Enquirer Post		ME	133	363
Sacramento	**803**			
Bee		M	181	350
Orlando	**812**			
Sentinel		A	164	341
Kansas City	**790**			
KC Star		M	131	347
San Antonio	**752**			
Express News		M	131	347
Las Vegas	**731**			
Review		ME	150	225
Columbus, O	**709**			
Dispatch		M	131	319
Indianapolis, IN	**688**			
Star		M	183	323
Charlotte	**676**			
Observer		M	136	353
Austin, TX	**651**			
		M	103	223
Am.Statesman				
Norfolk	**643**			
Virginia Pilot		M	130	256
Providence	**628**			
Journal		M	97	286
Milwaukee	**616**			
Journal-		M	176	347
Sentinel				

6
Digital

A Quick Digital Reference

*A synthesized reference for various internet
Advertising forms. Includes data on penetration, audiences,
usage, our exclusive 2014 market outlook,
and cost benchmarks.*

Digital

Media Availabilities

There are many ways to advertise on the internet. Some of the leading forms include:

- **The Website Itself** – A company's website is generally their single most important asset on the internet. The majority of internet marketing activities usually focus on driving the right people to the website.
- **Search Engine Optimization (SEO)** – Strategies and tactics employed to help the search engines find a site in a search, including work on the website itself and external activities which will raise a website's search rankings on Google, Yahoo, Bing, etc.
- **Paid Search** – Advertiser Pays search engines for key word traffic directed to Advertiser's website. ***Accounts for 47% of ad expenditures on the internet.***
- **Display Ads & Banners (23% of online spend)** – Advertisements and banners displayed on millions of websites. May be used to generate traffic to website or for branding purposes (effectiveness of display ads in branding is an open issue).
- **Email** – Commercial email is still an important channel, especially for CRM purposes. However, spam laws limit its use in creating new customers.
- **Blogs** – A form of social media, blogs are nearly free!
- **Mobile** – The fastest growing, albeit still small, form of internet advertising takes many forms—from texting to viewing videos and programs.
- **Social Media** – Social media have become a major advertising platform through membership activities and CPC advertising, e.g., advertisers can buy text ads targeted to certain groups, similar to Google or other PPC search engines.
- **Rich Media & Video** – Rich media and video are fast growing creative applications which increase internet ad effectiveness.

- **Gaming** – By advertising in games, some advertisers hope to build their image and relationship with highly targeted groups, especially young consumers.

Advantages

- Engagement with the consumer: All forms of internet advertising target highly selective audiences, people actually interested in product/service or offer
- Interactivity – Most advertising on the internet offers the potential for two-way communication with customers or website visitors.
- Metrics to measure results, including website visits, pages visited, time spent, conversion
- Customer Relationship Management (CRM) – communicate inducements, offers, private customer offers.
- Growing number of creative options.
- Flexible rate options (e.g., CPC vs. CPM)
- High reach potential

Disadvantages

- The focus of Internet advertising planning is primarily tactical (i.e., rather than strategic)
- The majority of internet ad investments are in CPC, classified, banners, not the strongest branding media.
- Difficulty in integration of offline and online media
- Determining the role of internet vs. traditional advertising, e.g., are display ads on websites the best choice for "branding"?
- Limited creative/message flexibility
- Limited branding potential?
- Email spamming laws

Market Outlook - Digital

- Overall internet ad expenditures are expected to increase at an above average rate (+10% or more in 2014)
- AOL will launch Ad-Tech "Upfront" believing that just like television, advertisers will commit budgets to machine traded advertising ahead of time (assuming they can get a better deal by doing so.)
- Look for increased internet ad rates in 2014, including CPC rates for paid search, display ads& banners, mobile, social
- Other media are forecast to increase by 1-2%
- This means that increased internet spending will come out of the budgets normally used for traditional media as political ads will drive even higher demand.
- However, the greatest growth will be in mobile media which could reach $15 billion.
- Search will continue to dominate internet ad spend with nearly 45% of the total, followed by display, social media, and rich media (which includes internet video), and classified ads.
- The internet user base also continued its growth according to research released by the TVB.
- Retail is the largest advertising business category for the internet, followed
- Performance based pricing will continue to raise its popularity over CPM based pricing.

Internet Reach Potential

- Internet reach continues to increase among all age groups
- High income persons are the most likely internet users
- Internet usage has increased in every group

"Reached Yesterday"	Adults	A25-54	HHI $75K+
2008	66%	75%	85%
2010	68	73	70
2012	73	76	82

Source; TVB/Nielsen Media Research, 2008-2012

Internet User Demographics

- Internet user demographics vary by where the net is used
- At work users are most upscale

	% Home Use	% Work Use	% Other Use
Men	49	50	48
College Grad	37	48	34
Age 18-34	34	33	58
Age 55+	22	15	12
Prof/Mgr	33	53	29
$75K+ HHI	36	42	27

Source: MRI, 2012

Share of Global Searches

- In April 2013, Google's market share dropped .6% to 67% while Bing increased .6% to 17% market share. Yahoo continued its slide down to 12% market share

	July 2005	July 2006	Aug 2009	2013
Google	46%	49%	68%	67%
Yahoo	23	24	8	12
MSN/Bing	13	10	3	17
AOL	5	6	1	1
Ask Network	2	3	1	2.4

Source:DoubleClick 2005-2009; NetMarketShare, 2011

Internet Ad Revenues

- Key word search largest method of internet advertising (43% of $)
- Display down to 19% of total vs. 22% in 2009

	2002	2006	2008	2009	2013E*
REVENUE (B)	**$6.0**	**$16.0**	**$21.9**	**$22.7**	**$41****
Keyword Search	15%	40%	41%	47%	43%
Display Ads	29	21	21	22	19
Sponsorship	18	4	3	2	4
Classifieds	15	20	17	10	6
Slotting Fees	8	<1	<1	<1	<1
Rich Media	5	6	8	11**	11**
Interstitial	5	-NA	NA-	NA-	NA-
Email	4	1	2	1	1
Lead Gen	NA	7	8	6	4

*First six months. ** Includes digital video. Data not comparable to prior years.
Source: IAB

Internet Ad Revenues by Business Category

- Source of internet ad revenues fairly stable since 2008
- One-fifth of revenues from retail
- How will these revenue patterns affect internet ad growth?

Category	2008	2009	2013E*
Retail	21%	20%	20%
Telecom	15	16	12
Financial Svs	13	12	13
Automotive	12	11	13
Computing	10	10	8
Consumer Pkg. Goods	7	6	5
Leisure/Travel	6	6	8
Entertainment	4	4	4
Health	4	4	6
Media	3	4	4

First six months Source: IAB.

Internet Revenues by Pricing Model

- The pay per click model continues to dominate
- CPM pricing has plummeted to 33% of total

	2006	2008	2009	2013*
CPM	48%	39%	37%	33%
Performance	47	57	59	65
Hybrid	5	4	4	2

* First six months 2013. Source: IAB *

Where do Internet Ad Budgets Come From?

Budget	2006	2008
Magazines/Print	20	32
WebsiteDevelopment	15	22
Direct Mail	16	17
Web Display Ads	6	15
Newspaper Ads	13	15
TV Advertising	13	13
Conferences	8	11
Affiliate Marketing	10	9
Radio	na	9

Source: SEMPO Advertiser Surveys, 2006 & 2008, latest available

Search

Search Engine Optimization (SEO)

- **Search engine optimization (SEO)** is the process of improving the visibility of a web site or a web page in search engines via the "natural" or un-paid ("organic" or "algorithmic") search results. Other forms of search engine marketing (SEM) target paid listings.

Paid Search

- Paid search involves paying a search engine like Google or Yahoo when someone in their audience is exposed to your ad or clicks on a link to your site (CPC/PPC)

Organic vs. Paid Search – One Benchmark

- 20 times more search engine traffic comes from organic search vs. paid
- Conversion rates highest from PPC traffic (average

Minimum Bids on Search Engines

- Most search engines require minimum bids
- Keep in mind that minimum bids may not generate clicks if bids result in very low rankings on search result pages

CPC Search Engine	Min. Bid	Comments
Google	.05	Few key words at $.05
Yahoo	.10	Distant second to Google
Bing	.05	A distant third
Miva	.01	Formerly FindWhat
7 Search	.01	Has 35 of top engines
Kanoodle	.05	Net Zero, Dog Pile

Source: 2020

Keyword Cost Trends

- The cost efficiency of CPC as a marketing tool is decreasing.
- CPC costs have risen significantly, roughly tripling since 2005
- Click through rates have decreased significantly
- Cost per conversion has more than doubled
- Key Trend: ROI declining? Implications?

Metric	2005	2007	2008	2010	2012
CPC	$.38	$.62	$.71	$1.24	$.84
CTR	1.5%	.3%	.3%	.7%	.5%
Avg Position	4.0	3.9	4.0	3.7	2.6
CPM	$5.56	$1.95	$2.16	$8.55	$4.03
Conversion %	3.8%	7.0%	7.5%	6.8%	3.4%
Cost/Conversion	$10.18	$6.41	$7.02	$13.14	$24.40

Estimated 2014 Ad Costs – Paid Search

- Expect CPCs to increase 20%+ in 2014
- Cheap mobile clicks have reduced overall click costs
- After experiencing lower revenue with increased clicks, Google has introduced Enhanced Campaigns and increased use of extensions.

Enter: Google Enhanced Campaigns

- Beginning in July 2013, Google changed the way advertisers can purchase Adwords ads which have run on desktop and mobile search results. Now, rather than separate prices for desk top and mobile, Google has conjoined the purchases into a program called Enhanced Campaigns which forces advertisers to place a desktop bid (for key word), then specify what percentage more or less they would be willing to pay to run those ads on mobile as well.
- Google clearly believes this will enhance its revenue and will buoy unacceptably low cost mobile ad prices.

Enhanced Campaigns with Extensions

- The stated purpose of encouraging the use of extensions is to give consumers more reasons to click.
- Extensions may be used on specify location, phone number, side links, App extensions (link to download)
- Extensions are FREE, pay Google only for clicks (up to two clicks per impression).
- Testing needed

Source: Hochman Consulting, 2012

Display Ads & Banners

Most Effective Ad Sizes

- Half banners & rectangles typically more effective than ads that frame the page such as leaderboards and skyscrapers
- Ads with rich media and video have highest impact
- Worst performance with simple flash

Display Ad Format	Aware Impact
Rectangle (180x150)	4.6%
Half Banner (234x60)	4.4
Medium Rectangle (200x250)	2.7
Large Rectangle (336x280)	2.3
Wide Skyscraper (160x600)	2.0
Leaderboard (728x90)	1.9
Skyscraper 120x600)	1.9

Half Page Ad 300x600)	1.8
Full Banner (468x60)	1.6
Button 120x90)	-0.6

Estimated Costs - Display Ads & Banners

- Display ads and banners may be purchased from individual website owners, networks, or exchanges.
- Display ads can be purchased on social networks, including You Tube, and portals such as AOL.
- May be purchased on a CPM basis or on a cost per click basis
- CPMs may be as little as a dollar or less to many dollars
- Rates may vary significantly by product category
- CPMs have declined as demand fell in 2009
- Except Food, Entertainment and Real Estate, the CPM rates for display ads have declined across industries in the last three quarters which is quite good news for online advertisers but not so good news for web publishers and blog
- However, recent demand appears to be increasing which will drive up prices
- The following is an example of real world CPMs for a variety of specific internet channels, ad types & sizes

Examples of Internet Display Ad Rates*

Website	Space Unit	Target	CPM
Facebook Premium Placement		Sex, age	$7.00
Facebook Marketplace		Sex, age	<2.00
MySpace Music Channel	728x90	Under 24	3.75
You Tube Video Search	Video	Key words	5.00
You Tube Pre Roll Auctn	Video	Keywords	15-25.00
You Tube	Roadblock		$400K/day
Value Click Network	300c250	Varies	$1.50
Value Click Pre Roll	Video	BT/CT	18.00
Collective Pre Roll	Video	BT/CT	10-16.00
Yahoo	Home Page		$600K/day
CBS March Madness	Ad		$70 CPM
Hulu	Video		$30+ CPM

AOL Homepage	Takeover		700K/day
AOL News	728x90		11-15.00
MSN Pre Roll	Video		$26.00
MSN Mail (ROS)		General	4.50
Wall Street Journal	Video		$75-100.00
Web MD	Ad		$40-60.00
Forbes.com	Interstitial		$90.00
Fast Company	Welcome ad		$125.00
ESPN Brand Channel	Ad		$22.00

Display CPM Benchmarks by Product Category

- CPMs also vary widely by product category/audience ad size/format, and timing (supply & demand)
- Take advantage of timing efficiencies when possible

	Q1, 2009	Q2, 2009	Q3. 2009
Automotive	17.25	15.33	12.47
Beauty/Fashion	4.30	3.73	3.22
Business	6.01	6.26	5.68
Entertainment	5.76	6.53	7.07
Living/Lifestyle	14.36	11.45	10.15
Moms & Parents	8.48	1245	10.19.
Real Estate	2.38	6.49	7.62
Sports	4.94	7.09	5.48
News	11.40	10.50	10.26
Food	1.50	3.63	6.94

Real World Online Ad Costs

- Web sales people & site owners love to talk about their rate card rates, but many/most rate cards aren't worth the paper they are written on.
- In actuality, online rates are open to negotiation. Also, package deals, up front commitments and budget promised help drive digital ad costs down. Following *__examples may or may not be achievable depending on market conditions.__*

- **Yahoo Homepage Takeover (Ask: $600K/Buy $450K)**
- **Facebook Log Out Screen (Ask: $700K/Buy $100K)**
- **Hulu InStream Ads (Ask: $30 CPM); Sell $25-30)**
- **Twitter Trending Topic (Ask: $120K; Sell $80K)**

Top 10 Social Media Sites

- Social media have grabbed the spotlight. Following are the top 10 sites.
- In addition to consumer interaction opportunities, most also accept cost per click advertising.

Site	Unique Visitors	% Reach	Avg. Minutes	Ads Available
Facebook	160.7	73%	438	CPC
Twitter	40.3	18	41	CPC
LinkedIn	37.3	17	21	CPC
Tumblr	26.9	12	168	NA
Myspace	26.8	12	6	CPC/Ads
Pinterest	23.3	11	55	No CPC
MyLife	10.6	5	2	Available
Yahoo Profile	10.5	4.8	2	Available
MeetMe Media	8.0	4	82	Display
GoodReads	7.1	3	8	CPC

Source: Advertising Age, 2020

Cost of Social Media

What does social media advertising/marketing cost? According to one social media agency, there are two primary cost areas: staff time and CPC ads:

1. **Staff Costs (e.g., example of managementfees)**
   - Twitter (to $7500/month)
   - Facebook (to $9000/month)
   - Strategy Development ($3000-15000/month)
2. **Cost of ads**
   - Clicks CPC ads
   - Website display ads

Online Video

- Online video costs are all over the board and in many cases are significantly higher than traditional television.
- Make sure to compare availabilities based on the same commercial length, for video ads, usually :15
- Does online video warrant paying a cost efficiency premium? The following table suggests than the CPM for online video could be 5-7 times higher than primetime television.
- Important to negotiate prices with vendors

Examples of Online Video Costs

Source	CPM Range
Web Video Report (8 sites)	$20-40.00
Meta Cafe	$10-35.00
Pre Roll	35.00
No Good TV	$15-40.00
My Space (:15 in music section + static ad)	$25.00
Wall Street Journal	$90.00
Hulu	$30-45.00
You Tube	CPM low as $1.00-- if commit to $100K on Google within 90 days
TELEVISION (primetime :15 CPM adults)	**$5.00**

Mobile

Growth of Mobile Advertising (MM)

- Search has replaced SMS as #1 in mobile ad dollars
- Search/Display are extensions of basics, e.g., Adwords

Year	SMS	Display	Search	Total
2009	$226	$206	$59	$491
2011	325	554	307	1,190
2012	390	652	548	1,590
2013E	468	714	954	2,140

Source:Bia/Kelsey, eMarketer, Lightspeed Research

- Wondering about running mobile ads in AdWords (or other search engines)? Google AdWords released a mobile research study that concluded *88 percent of ad clicks from mobile search are incremental to organic clicks.* In other words, the paid clicks aren't replaced by organic clicks when search ads are paused.
- Mobile ads appear on mobile devices in Google search results, on content websites, in apps, etc.

Mobile Ad Formats

- **Mobile ads available in a variety of formats, e.g.:**
  - SMS Messages (most common)
  - Clickable banners
  - Text links
  - Tenancies
  - Pre roll video

Smart Phone Users (115K)

- Downloaded/streamed video last mo.	19%
- Watched YouTube	25
- Podcasting	2

Mobile Ad Costs

- Mobile competes for key words vs. desk top

- Mobile ads sold on CPM or CPC basis, similar to other distribution and distribution outlets appear to be 60-90% lower than the same desktop key word costs

- Mobile key word costs

- As The New York Times reported, Google sells mobile ads/clicks for half to two-thirds as much as desktop ads, but the mobile ads are only a third as effective

- Online advertising company (Turn) reports a 15% increase in display ad costs and a 45% drop in mobile

- Why are mobile ads so cheap?

Email

Permission Email

- Mail to customers or people who have asked to receive mail
- Follow the law!
- Spam is frowned upon
- Represents a reported 1% of internet ad expenditures
- Believe a lot of local email spending is not measured
- Is email an effective marketing tool?

Benchmarks/Metrics

- Email performance is highly variable, depending on the mailing list, the message, and the effectiveness of the creative.

  That said, here are some overall benchmarks for email performance:

Avg. Delivery	94.8%
Open Rates:	22.1
Click Thru	5.3
House List:	20% open/6.4% CTR

Email Costs

Email costs include list cost, if any, creative development if any, transmission, and list management

- List costs up to $300+ CPM for a purchased list to zero for your owned customer or newsletter list
- Creative costs can range from $50-150+ per hour
- DIY sources for developing and sending emails include dozens of companies like Constant Contact and Graphic Mail which provide creative templates, sending, and some post analysis of met

7
Other Media

A Guide to Other Media
Outdoor, direct mail and non-traditional media. Audience data, research and creative media ideas.

Out of Home

Diverse Availabilities…

- **Billboards – Majority of Outdoor Avails**
    - 30 sheet posters (10x22), usually in town
    - 8 sheet (5x11`), often on buildings, ethnic areas
    - Bulletins (size from 10x25 to 20x60)
        - May be permanent or rotating
        - Illuminated for night visibility or not
    - Digital bulletins
- **Street Furniture**
    - Bench (2x6)
- **Transit**
    - Transit Shelter (5.5x4)
    - Bus (King = 2.5x12)
- **Alternative**
    - Mall (5x4)
    - Kiosks
- **Spectaculars**
    - If you can dream it you can probably do it!
    - Example: Times Square, Goodyear Tire in Detroit

Advantages of Billboards

- 98% reach potential
- Geographic targeting
- Variety of sizes and locations
- Help to create simple awareness, e.g., of name
- New "Eyes On" research methodology goes beyond traffic counts to audience exposure.

Disadvantages of Billboards

- Even the largest outdoor boards often look like postage stamps to passing traffic because they are so far away
- Majority of people passing an outdoor board do not notice

Limited communication possible/many advertisers do not follow the KISS principle

- A large part of the weakness of outdoor as an advertising medium is not the fault of the medium; it is the fault of the creative developed for outdoor.

- Much of the outdoor creative is ineffective due to too many words, complicated graphics, too much to assimilate in a fraction of a second!

Weekly Reach

Drivers/Passengers	96%
Pedestrians	79
Commuters	64

Outdoor Market Outlook

- Growth in outdoor revenues is projected at 2-5% in 2014
- Long term growth likely as there are so many forms of OOH
- Placed based media could grow20-25%
- The new "Eyes On" research with more granular data could help spur buying
- Digital billboard availabilities should reach 3700 by 2014, selling at 2-3 times higher CPM than traditional bulletins.

Estimated 2014 Billboard Costs

DMAs	% US HH	Cost 100 TRPS Rotary Bulletins	Cost 100 TRPS 30 Sheet
Top 10	32.8	$2660	$1431
Top 20	46.9	3900	1550
Top 30	56.4	4665	1870
Top 40	63.5	5250	2100
Top 50	69.3	5700	2300
Top 60	74.2	6140	2450
Top 70	78.0	6450	2575
Top 80	81.4	6750	2700
Top 90	84.3	6990	2800
Top 100	87.1	7250	2900

Rotary Bulletins

- Following table shows the number of boards, circulation (millions), the four week cost, CPM and reach and frequency for a showing in several major markets
- Target: General market
- 100 Adult GRPS per day

Market	# Faces	4 wk Circ	4 wk Cost	CPM	R	F
Atlanta	53	88.3	$156.4	$1.77	87%	32
Chicago	134	175.6	670.0	3.82	88	32
Dallas/Ft. Worth	30	84.8	204.0	2.40	88	32
Houston	40	110.0	184.0	1.66	87	32
Los Angeles	253	355.6	1986.0	5.58	87	32
New York (subs)	17	21.3	238.0	11.51	87	32
Philadelphia	84	135.7	514.1	4.12	88	34
San Francisco	82	137.3	1492.0	3.58	88	32
Washington/Balt.	149	123.4	750.4	7.91	88	32

Source: ClearChannel

"Eyes On" Research

Historically, the advertising community has viewed outdoor audiences with justified skepticism. Now, the outdoor industry appears to be getting its act together with audience research which surpasses what is available for most other media. The data, from the Traffic Audit Bureau (TAB) provides not only reach & frequency estimates, but also estimates of how many eyeballs actually were on the ad.

(Source: 2020 opinion)

Direct Mail

Advantages

- **Targeting** – unsurpassed ability to target consumers on almost any set of criteria – purchasing behavior, demographics, psychographics, etc.
- **Message** - Flexible message format can tell lengthy story
- **Response** – Highly suited to promotions and offers
- **Results** - Immediate & measured results

Disadvantages

- Compared to traditional media or internet
- Quality of mailing lists vary widely
- Direct mail response variables are complex and require much analysis; many practitioners lack the knowledge to implement effective direct mail programs; common sense solutions may not work.
- Consequently, not all direct mail programs achieve the response goals.
- Mail clutter & consumer resistance

Estimated Costs

- The cost of direct mail programs varies widely due to the particular mailing package, postage utilized, the cost of the list, whether the mailing is solo or shared with other advertisers. Following are some benchmark costs:

CPM	Solo	Coop	Total
List cost	0-$300+ NA	$300	---
Mailing package	250-5000	NA	100
Postage	440 -2900+*	NA	440*
Mail House	25	NA	NA
Fulfillment	25	NA	NA
Total	**840-$8000+**	**400+**	**$540-840**

Assumes first class postage (normally recommended).   Postcard is jumbo size

Non Traditional Media

3D Printing

3D printing literally allows advertisers to print a 3D image rather than the typical two dimensional image. 3D printing was a novelty just two years ago, but the technology has become increasingly prominent not just in manufacturing -- as a way to actually produce physical products -- but also as a neat marketing tool for brands.

Clients are incorporating 3D printing into their branding efforts in various ways, some fun and gimmicky and some quite useful. For example, on one end of the spectrum we recently saw an effort out of Israel for Coca-Cola that used 3D printing in a contest that created consumer mini-me's. On the other end was a Belgian insurance brand that leveraged the technology to solve one of its customers' most annoying problems.

Advertorials
- Advertorials are advertising sponsored sections in magazines, newspapers, or on the web which focus on a specific topic or audience interest. An advertorial section could deal with the results of testing new cars, an analysis of the best smart phone options, cooking lite or thousands of other ideas.
- The advertising premise would be that associated ads could better engage the audience in a highly relevant environment.

Barter
- Companies with excess inventories may find it advantageous to trade those inventories for advertising time or space. Advertising media is one of the largest categories of business barter.
- One can barter directly with individual media to trade inventory for time or space. For example, a company may

be able to trade office equipment to a radio station in exchange for an appropriate amount of advertising on the station.

- Or, one can work through a reputable barter house which does business with many media. While the barter house must be paid a commission for transactions, this approach provides the greatest number of potential barter deals.

"Buzz" Marketing

- Based on the principle of word of mouth, "buzz marketing" takes it to a whole new level through a well-planned campaign to get people talking about the product.
- Buzz marketing may involve recruiting people to promote a product or service in popular bars or events. For example, a motorcycle manufacturer hired models to ride their bikes to trendy bars and clubs in Los Angeles where they would strike up conversations with other patrons.
- Another example: a toy company hired fourth and fifth graders to act as "secret agents"

Event Marketing

- Event marketing is one of the fastest growing areas of marketing communications. Event marketing uses a variety of sports and entertainment venues to promote their products. For example, the auto companies display their products at annual auto shows in larger markets.
- Companies also display and explain their products at sporting events, fairs and festivals, air shows, and wherever large crowds of people congregate.
- Typically, sponsorship of an event will include a sponsorship fee paid to the promoter for rights and space and activation costs to cover the cost of tents, personnel to man the exhibit, premium giveaways, and so on.

Flyers

- Sometimes we overlook the most obvious opportunities. Advertising flyers, delivered to the front door of prospects, can be a highly targeted, inexpensive medium-- especially for small businesses who can have flyers distributed to the homes in their Retail Trading Area.

Gas Station TV

- Gas Station TV provides advertisers with an additional opportunity to have their commercials viewed while people are standing at the gas pump. (gasstationtv.com)

Google Enhanced Campaigns

- In July 2013, Google introduced its new enhanced campaigns program, an update to Adwords
- Notion of "device unification" combining devices for desktop. Smart phones and tablets
- Buyer places keyword bids based on desktop CPCs and indicates what percentage more or less buyer will pay for The key words on mobile
- Extensions (such as phone numbers) may also be inserted into ads

Home Shopping Networks

- QVC and HSN are huge channels of distribution for many companies. In fact, some companies sell their goods ONLY through the home shopping networks.
- To sell through these channels, they will first evaluate the product for promotion on a program.
- If acceptable to the network, there is no time cost to the advertiser.
- The products most likely to be accepted are those with a mass market and which demonstrate well, and are topical or timely.

Hot Air Balloons

- What would you be willing to pay for an ad on the front cover of a magazine? Your logo on hot air balloons could create some buzz and free press exposure. Check out adventureballoon.com.

In-Store

- Reaching people at the point of sale can be extremely effective. There are many media opportunities to reach in-store shoppers, including merchandising displays, shelf talkers, next purchase coupons, coupons on cash register tapes, in store video and audio, product sampling, ads on shopping carts and more...all intended to stimulate immediate impulse purchasing.

Micro-Encapsulation

- If your product appeals to the sense of smell, consider micro-encapsulation of the odor to gain purchase consideration. Perfumes, new car smell, or the smell of baking cookies can be powerful communications tools.

Opportunistic Buying

- Advertising time and space are perishable; yesterday's unsold spot in NCIS has no value. A significant amount of time and space goes unsold.
- To capitalize on the opportunity, many buyers hold back a portion of their budgets to capitalize on distress selling at a fraction of the normal rate. They make immediate buying decisions.
- It is smart to advise media and reps that you are interested in fire sale opportunities (however, be warned that if you never buy anything, you will be off the list of fire sale prospects.)

Product Placement

- Product placement involves getting a product shown or featured in a television program or a movie. For example, Chevrolet might want the Corvette portrayed as a tough and fast sports car hero in a film which emphasizes scenes involving speed, handling agility, and plain old coolness.

- Product placement is also one of the fastest growing areas of marketing communication.

Publicity

- You can create free publicity if you have something worth saying about your product.
- Publicity may take the form of newsworthy articles in magazines, newspapers, broadcast media, or online.
- Getting free publicity requires a proactive approach to creating interesting newsworthy content.
- Consider staging PR events which will generate press coverage on its own, e.g., a boat manufacturer may sponsor a boat race, given their reputation for superior technology, with prizes to winners.

Custom Publishing

- Custom publishing is another growing area of marketing communications. Many companies publish owner magazines as part of their CRM efforts. Allstate's Friend's magazine is an example; AAA publishes a localized travel magazine for its members. Financial institutions utilize newsletters published on and off line.

Remnants

- Remnants are the unsold time and space in the various media vehicles. These may often be purchased for a small fraction of the retail price.
- There are a variety of companies which specialize in selling remnant space in broadcast, print, and online media.

Sampling

- Sometimes products don't sell because consumers don't know how good it is or because a new product is truly superior.

- When the product sells itself, it may be sampled in stores, by mailed samples, at events, direct mail or other means.
- Example: auto companies display their vehicles and offer test drives at events where product specialists answer questions.

Shared Mail Packages

- There are many opportunities to participate in shared mail packages with companies who print and distribute the packages: Valassis, ADVO, and many others. Cost of the mailing is shared by participating advertisers with a price tag much lower than a solo mailing

Leverage Sponsorships

- Sponsor a television special or series in which your product is the hero of the program. Examples:
- A Chevrolet Camaro was the hero of the television series as the car obeyed its owner's commands.
- If you sell beauty aids, consider a beauty show or beauty contests.
- Or, Crock Pot could sponsor a cooking show using the product.

Theatre Screen

- Advertising on movie screens is available on a national, regional, or local market basis.
- Offerings typically include cinema spot advertising, slides, lobby and concessional promotions,
- May be targeted geographically and by target audience
- Large screen format may require special production on 35MM film to ensure quality.
- Screenvision is the largest seller of cinema advertising.

Wraps of Vehicles or Buildings

- Need high visual impact? Light on words?
- Vehicle wraps involve "wrapping" a vehicle – car, truck, bus—with a highly graphic message

- Wraps are even possible in high-rise office buildings, e.g., Chrysler uses highly impactful wraps on their office building in Michigan.

Websites - Local Search

- **Yelp.com** is a community website that connects users to the things that are great in their neighborhood. The site originated in San Francisco, but has evolved to include areas across the country. Find recommendations for restaurants, shopping, beauty, doctors and more on Yelp.com. **Yext.com** also provides local businesses with opportunity to reach local customers who are searching for something specific in their mar

8

Top 100 Market Planner

"The Odds of hitting your target go up dramatically when you aim at it."
The Thumbnail Media Planner is a top 100 market Reference for geographic targeting

Rank	DMA	12+ Pop	HHs	% US TV HH
58	Albany-Schen-Troy	1293.5	551.1	0.5%
45	Albuquerque/Santa Fe	1746.8	710.1	0.6%
9	Atlanta	6316.9	2292.6	2.0%
47	Austin	1743	686.8	0.6%
27	Baltimore	2720.1	1097.3	1.0%
94	Baton Rouge	829.6	333	0.3%
39	Birmingham, AL	1764.4	738.8	0.6%
7	Boston	5983.8	2379.7	2.1%
51	Buffalo	1494	645.2	0.6%
95	Burlington/Plattsburg	781.6	323.8	0.3%
89	Cedar Rapids/Waterloo	817.5	344.2	0.3%
82	Champaign/Spring/Dec	891.3	386.2	0.3%
98	Charleston, SC	752.5	311.3	0.3%
65	Charleston/Huntington	1159.3	465.0	0.4%
25	Charlotte	2828.2	1140.9	1.0%
86	Chattanooga	883	366.8	0.3%
3	Chicago	9381.5	3493.5	3.4%
35	Cincinnati	2261.7	896.1	0.8%
18	Cleveland/Ak/Canton	3668.7	1514.2	1.3%
90	Colorado Springs/Pueb	841.7	343.2	0.3%
77	Columbia, SC	953.6	404.8	0.4%
32	Columbus, OH	2178.8	932.7	0.8%
5	Dallas/FW	6786.3	2571.3	2.2%
100	Davenport/Roci Is.	732.8	307.1	0.3%
63	Dayton	1141.9	493.6	0.4%
17	Denver	3839.4	1548.6	1.4%
72	Des Moines	1029.8	431.3	0.4%
11	Detroit	4758	1842.7	1.6%
91	El Paso	920.5	336.6	0.3%
68	Flint/Saginaw	1112.9	451.9	0.4%
55	Fresno	1817.6	574.8	0.5%
62	Ft Myers	1159.0	504.2	0.4%

Market Planner

%Cable	%ADS	%<18	%18-34	35-64	%55+	AA Rank	Hisp Rank	Wh Collar
76	18	23	22	30	25	86	97	74
37	46	30	21	30	19	107	12	73
57	38	26	25	32	17	2	21	69
60	27	26	28	30	17	71	22	71
74	21	24	23	32	21	11	62	73
71	25	29	24	29	18	32	123	69
48	46	25	22	30	23	18	83	68
86	13	23	24	30	22	28	24	96
63	30	24	21	19	26	63	87	69
52	40	25	24	30	21	161	161	71
57	31	25	23	18	24	126	135	70
58	35	25	23	29	24	89	127	72
63	29	26	23	30	20	48	122	73
53	42	25	21	30	24	118	158	71
57	37	25	23	31	21	14	38	61
59	34	25	21	31	21	81	90	61
62	29	26	23	30	20	3	6	70
57	29	27	22	30	21	35	91	69
69	25	25	21	30	24	16	57	68
44	44	27	24	30	19	108	41	72
51	40	27	24	30	19	25	106	70
67	22	26	24	30	20	36	75	72
49	35	27	25	31	17	9	5	70
55	34	26	19	30	25	123	94	65
60	25	26	21	30	23	62	130	67
49	41	26	23	33	17	59	15	71
46	38	25	21	29	25	123	93	73
69	22	26	23	31	21	7	44	69
43	32	33	24	27	17	128	16	68
61	30	27	22	30	21	73	104	70
36	47	32	23	27	18	94	14	71
63	33	20	17	26	38	85	34	73

Rank	DMA	12+ Pop	HHs	% US TV HH
42	Grand Rapids	1878.8	722.2	0.6%
69	Green Bay	1061.4	445.8	0.4%
46	Greensboro	1644.4	691.2	0.6%
37	Greenville/Spart	2039.5	860.9	0.8%
99	Greenville-New Bern	685.6	307.6	0.3%
87	Harlingen/Wslco	1174.7	361.8	0.3%
41	Harrisburg/Lanc/York	1820.5	729.4	0.6%
30	Hartford/NH	2472.1	1006.3	0.9%
71	Honolulu	1215	434.7	0.4%
10	Houston	5883.5	2185.3	1.9%
80	Huntsville/Decatur	937.4	394.0	0.3%
26	Indianapolis	2704.5	1109.9	1.0%
93	Jackson MS	852.7	334.5	0.3%
50	Jacksonville	1673.5	669.8	0.6%
31	Kansas City	2298	939.7	0.8%
61	Knoxville	1279.5	527.8	0.5%
40	Las Vegas	1889.4	737.3	0.6%
64	Lexington	1179.2	488.9	0.4%
56	Little Rock	1345.7	571.6	0.5%
2	Los Angeles	17036.5	5569.8	4.8%
48	Louisville	1595.9	674.1	0.6%
85	Madison	898	378.3	0.3%
49	Memphis	1676	669.9	0.6%
16	Miami/FL	4104	1583.8	1.4%
34	Milwaukee	2183.6	907.7	0.8%
15	Minneapolis/SP	4283.5	1721.9	1.5%
60	Mobile/Pensacola	1303.9	527.9	0.5%
29	Nashville	2483.9	1024.6	0.9%
52	New Orleans	1613.5	643.7	0.6%
1	New York	20093.4	73587.8	6.4%
43	Norfolk/Port/NP	1761.5	718.8	0.6%
44	Oklahoma City	1662.4	712.6	0.6%

Market Planner

%Cable	%ADS	%<18	%18-34	%35-64	%55+	AA Rank	Hisp Rank	Wh Collar
57	31	28	23	29	20	72	59	64
51	30	27	21	29	23	158	107	63
58	35	23	22	32	23	26	53	63
45	48	23	21	31	25	30	65	63
52	39	26	23	30	21	54	102	70
41	33	37	21	24	18	172	10	72
68	25	24	22	30	24	78	64	66
42	32	23	23	31	23	84	16	71
90	7	25	23	31	21	105	66	75
55	29	29	24	31	16	8	4	69
57	37	25	22	31	22	67	98	62
60	28	26	23	30	21	31	58	69
40	53	29	22	28	22	40	53	71
58.9	34.6	26	23	30	21	27	60	19
62	26	26	22	30	21	37	47	72
58	35	24	21	31	24	96	110	68
60	32	25	23	32	20	56	23	72
49	44	25	24	30	21	88	114	67
42	49	26	21	29	24	38	89	69
52	37	27	26	30	18	6	1	70
61	29	26	21	31	22	55	86	67
51	33	25	24	30	21	121	101	70
50	41	28	22	29	21	13	78	68
70	26	22	21	30	27	12	3	74
60	19	26	22	30	22	40	42	67
54	28	27	23	30	20	49	46	71
53	40	27	22	39	22	34	99	96
57	36	25	23	31	21	29	55	69
58	36	29	22	29	20	20	63	72
84	14	23	23	31	23	1	2	74
69	24	27	22	29	18	15	72	72
54	31	26	23	29	22	61	52	70

Rank	DMA	12+ Pop	HHs	% US TV HH
76	Omaha	1006.7	415.5	0.4%
19	Orlando/Daytona	3561.5	1465.5	1.3%
81	Paducah/CG	920.4	393.3	0.3%
4	Philadelphia	7445	2993.4	2.6%
13	Phoenix	4982.4	1811.3	1.6%
23	Pittsburgh	2663.6	1171.5	1.0%
22	Portland ,OR	2994.4	1190.0	1.0%
78	Portland, ME	942.9	401.4	0.4%
53	Providence/NB	1512.7	620.0	0.5%
24	Raleigh/Durham	2726.1	1143.4	1.0%
57	Richmond	1334.9	559.4	0.5%
66	Roanoke	1047.3	455.9	0.4%
79	Rochester NY	956.2	398.8	0.4%
20	Sacramento/Stock	3838	1388.6	1.2%
33	Salt Lake City	2826.5	927.5	0.8%
36	San Antonio	2259.4	880.7	0.8%
28	San Diego	2889	1077.6	0.9%
6	San Francisco/Oak/SJ	6718.8	2506.5	2.2%
92	Savannah	796.7	335.1	0.3%
12	Seattle/Tacoma	4992.8	1811.4	1.6%
83	Shreveport	944.7	386.2	0.3%
97	South Bend/Elk	847.8	322.1	0.3%
73	Spokane	1030.6	426.7	0.4%
75	Springfield,MO	996.7	423.0	0.4%
21	St. Louis	3048.9	1253.9	1.0%
84	Syracuse	924.6	386.1	0.3%
14	Tampa/St. Pete	4177.9	1788.2	1.6%
74	Toledo	1011.1	426.3	0.4%
96	Tri Cities, TN/VA	754.7	323.6	0.3%
70	Tucson	1142.9	442.0	0.4%
59	Tulsa	1285.7	529.1	0.5%
88	Waco/Temple	875.4	353.2	0.3%
8	Washington DC	5935.9	2360.2	2.1%
38	West Palm Beach	1820.2	788.0	0.7%
67	Wichita	1118.8	454.9	0.4%
54	Wilkes Barre/Scranton	1401.1	590.7	0.5%

Market Planner

%Cable	%ADS	%<18	%18-34	%35-64	%55+	AA Rank	Hisp Rank	Wh Collar
70	21	27	26	29	22	92	70	72
67	27	23	22	29	27	21	17	72
38	55	24	20	29	27	97	140	68
80	16	24	22	30	24	5	18	72
46	41	27	22	29	22	53	8	70
70	24	22	21	29	28	51	108	72
56	31	26	20	32	21	87	31	67
69	23	35	21	31	23	147	146	72
87	9	23	23	29	25	84	51	68
54	37	25	25	30	19	10	35	70
57	34	24	23	32	21	23	81	71
40	50	22	22	31	25	58	129	64
70	19	23	27	28	22	75	84	73
51	41	28	23	30	20	41	11	71
43	40	37	22	25	16	122	29	69
57	31	29	22	28	20	68	7	73
79	15	25	27	29	19	64	13	72
65	29	23	24	33	20	19	9	72
59	37	28	25	27	20	45	96	69
73	21	25	23	32	20	46	27	72
36	57	28	20	28	24	33	88	68
43	39	27	21	29	23	95	80	61
41	45	27	21	30	23	146	74	70
32	51	24	20	29	27	137	119	69
51	39.9	26	21	30	23	17	73	72
76	17	25	25	29	22	101	128	71
80	14	20	18	27	34	22	19	73
64	25	27	22	29	22	80	78	64
56	39	23	20	32	25	134	156	64
48	41	26	23	28	23	108	25	71
48	39	26	20	30	24	77	67	5
54	38	27	29	25	19	70	43	71
72	24	24	24	34	18	4	20	76
73	26	20	18	27	35	43	28	75
61	29	27	21	28	24	100	54	67
63	32	23	20	29	28	115	85	68

DMA	$110-50K HH	$40-100K HH	$100+ HH	TV CPP HH
Albany-Schen-Troy	60	34	6	60
Albuquerque/Santa Fe	66	29	6	122
Atlanta	55	36	9	660
Austin	51	35	14	158
Baltimore	41	34	24	330
Baton Rouge	57	34	9	74
Birmingham, AL	62	31	7	70
Boston	43	41	16	735
Buffalo	65	31	4	100
Burlington/Plattsburg	62	33	5	73
Cedar Rapids/Waterloo	60	34	6	42
Champaign/Spring/Dec	59	35	6	41
Charleston, SC	36	28	36	50
Charleston/Huntington	69	27	4	56
Charlotte	60	33	7	126
Chattanooga	66	29	5	59
Chicago	44	41	15	1163
Cincinnati	52	38	10	130
Cleveland/Ak/Canton	57	35	8	295
Colorado Springs/Pueb	66	29	5	70
Columbia SC	64	31	5	49
Columbus, O	55	36	9	170
Dallas/FW	49	37	13	900
Davenport/Rock Is.	60	35	5	58
Dayton	55	37	8	52
Denver	53	37	10	304
Des Moines	60	34	7	58
Detroit	49	40	12	378
El Paso	72	24	4	89
Flint/Saginaw	632	33	5	44
Fresno	68	27	5	114
Ft Myers/Naples	62	29	9	98

Market Planner

TV CPP A25–54	A25-54 Cable CPP	Radio CPP	Key Nwspr Circ (000)	Key Newsp Cost 31.5"	Avg Bulletin Mo Cost
90	103	$50	115	15.6	n/a
180	209	45	72	5.0	1/6
990	1140	155	208	25.9	4/0
237	270	80	102	8.4	1.6
495	570	130	160	13.9	2.5
111	64	38	6.5	2.5	n/a
105	61	52	88.0	6.2	1.6
1100	1250	275	430.0	47.0	12.2
150	170	52	128.0	10.8	n/a
110	64	30	52.0	6.5	n/a
63	37	29	56.0	6.4	n/a
61	35	24	61.0	6.5	n/a
74	43	32	66.0	6.5	n/a
84	48	36	115.0	8.0	n/a
189	2000	98	125.0	13.0	2.5
88	100	27	58.0	3.0	n/a
1745	621	300	1100.0	115.0	5.0
190	218	85	146.0	16.6	2.1
325	375	100	373.0	24.0	3.3
104	60	35	55.0	6.5	n/a
73	43	30	60.0	6.2	n/a
255	295	75	120.0	12.5	2.1
1350	1555	475	420.0	45.0	6.8
87	50	25	48.2	6.5	n/a
78	46	47	121.0	7.8	n/a
456	265	143	248.0	15.1	3.5
86	50	31	80.0	10.5	n/a
567	652	150	365.0	31.8	4.0
133	77	33	54.0	5.5	n/a
66	38	22	75.0	6.8	n/a
171	99	77	88.0	9.0	n/a
147	85	42	60.0	10.0	n/a

DMA	$110-50K HH	$40-100K HH	$100+ HH	TV CPP HH
Grand Rapids	56	37	7	92
Green Bay	60	35	5	51
Greensboro	66	29	5	52
Greenville/Spart	67	28	4	70
Greenville-New Bern	41	25	34	0
Harlingen/Wslco	75	20	4	84
Harrisburg/Lanc/York	53	39	8	118
Hartford/NH	44	43	13	240
Honolulu	49	40	11	82
Houston	49	36	15	1000
Huntsville/Decatur	61	33	6	55
Indianapolis	55	36	9	184
Jackson MS	63	30	7	40
Jacksonville	60	33	7	72
Kansas City	55	36	9	134
Knoxville	67	27	6	105
Las Vegas	58	34	8	256
Lexington	66	28	6	56
Little Rock	67	28	5	96
Los Angeles	51	37	12	2975
Louisville	60	33	7	104
Madison	57	35	7	48
Memphis	61	32	8	104
Miami/FL	60	31	8	1147
Milwaukee	53	39	8	143
Minneapolis/SP	52	39	10	350
Mobile/Pensacola	64	30	6	118
Nashville	58	33	9	157
New Orleans	62	31	7	112
New York	45	38	17	2627
Norfolk/Port/NP	64	31	4	140
Oklahoma City	68	28	5	98

Market Planner

TV CPP A25–54	Cable CPP	Radio CPP	Key Nwspr Circ (000)	Key Newsp Cost 31.5"	Avg Bulletin Mo Cost
138	80	40	121.0	8.1	1.7
77	45	33	72.0	6.9	n/a
78	45	$60	50.0	4.2	1.5
105	61	46	80.0	7.5	1.9
0	0	33	50.0	6.5	n/a
126	73	33	25.0	2.1	n/a
177	103	46	56.0	2.5	1.7
360	415	80	20.0	19.0	2.5
125	144	29	89.0	8.8	n/a
1500	1700	260	293.0	26.8	4.6
82	48	33	78.8	6.4	n/a
275	317	65	146.0	12.3	3.8
60	35	24	50.0	6.7	n/a
108	63	58	190.0	18.7	n/a
200	231	80	160.0	20.0	2.1
155	180	38	92.0	6.8	n/a
384	440	73	120.0	8.5	2.8
85	49	28	88.0	6.6	n/a
147	168	35	142.0	9.0	n/a
4460	5100	665	1368.0	110.4	8.0
150	172	47	160.0	12.1	1.4
72	42	36	69.0	4.0	n/a
152	175	52	97.6	10.8	2.7
2600	3000	178	368.0	36.2	3.7
210	250	63	147.0	13.2	3.2
525	625	130	388.0	20.8	5.5
170	200	35	160	11.5	n/a
225	265	70	103.0	13.0	2.1
175	205	63	115.0	7.2	n/a
3900	4450	600	2214.0	196.0	20.0
210	250	73	115.0	6.5	1.6
145	166	50	111.0	13.9	1.5

DMA	$110-50K HH	$40-100K HH	$100+ HH	TV CPP HH
Omaha	52	52	12	97
Orlando/Daytona	63	30	6	400
Paducah/CG	71	25	4	39
Philadelphia	46	40	14	742
Phoenix	64	30	6	426
Pittsburgh	58	33	9	253
Portland ,O	57	35	8	222
Portland, ME	62	33	5	75
Providence/NB	54	38	7	81
Raleigh/Durham	59	34	7	142
Richmond	57	36	7	120
Roanoke	69	27	4	75
Rochester NY	57	37	6	90
Sacramento/Stock	56	36	8	408
Salt Lake City	59	35	6	267
San Antonio	54	40	6	185
San Diego	52	37	11	340
San Francisco/Oak/SJ	38	40	23	1133
Savannah	69	26	5	95
Seattle/Tacoma	46	39	16	464
Shreveport	68	27	5	62
South Bend/Elk	61	34	6	33
Spokane	77	29	5	69
Springfield,MO	74	22	4	45
St. Louis	54	38	9	245
Syracuse	64	32	4	67
Tampa/St. Pete	65	28	7	640
Toledo	58	36	6	55
Tri Cities, TN/VA	70	26	4	41
Tucson	69	26	5	90
Tulsa	67	28	5	62
Waco/Temple	68	27	5	74
Washington DC	41	42	17	1035
West Palm Beach	55	33	12	111
Wichita	64	31	5	64
Wilkes Barre/Scranton	65	30	5	61

Market Planner

TV CPP A25–54	Cable CPP	Radio CPP	Key Nwspr Circ (000)	Key Newsp Cost 31.5"	Avg Bulletin Mo Cost
148	170	37	115.0	6.8	n/a
600	700	108	160.0	13.2	3.8
59	34	20	64.0	6.5	n/a
1115	1300	270	488.0	45.1	6.1
638	370	155	252.0	19.3	4.5
380	450	89	276.0	19.1	2.4
333	393	120	224.0	13.3	2.7
112	65	40	40.0	3.2	n/a
122	71	70	98.0	13.4	n/a
212	123	90	106.0	8.6	2.5
180	220	52	95.0	8.0	n/a
112	130	38	126.0	6.6	n/a
135	155	40	106.0	17.0	n/a
602	710	105	160.0	12.5	5.5
350	412	80	142.0	9.5	1.9
278	161	75	106.0	13.0	3.6
510	610	142	237.0	20.8	2.6
1700	2000	470	480.0	65.0	6.0
130	155	17	54.0	6.5	n/a
680	780	150	304.0	26.0	4.5
93	54	24	62.0	6.4	n/a
50	29	26	51.0	6.5	n/a
100	120	24	68.0	6.5	n/a
68	40	25	66/0	6/5	n/a
365	435	88	162	27.5	2.7
95	115	41	69.0	8.0	n/a
920	1050	110	308.0	40.8	3.5
80	95	28	90.0	5.3	n/a
62	36	29	53.0	6.5	n/a
140	165	41	73.0	7.9	n/a
92	110	45	79.0	4.3	n/a
111	64	41	57.0	6.4	n/a
1550	1800	270	500.0	28.8	6.6
160	190	67	101.0	7.0	1.7
91	105	27	60.0	5.1	n/a
92	53	36	66.0	7.5	n/a

9

Emerging Markets

- **Baby Boomers**
- **U.S. Hispanic Market**
- **African Americans**
- **Asian Americans**

Baby Boomer Trends

What are Baby Boomers?
- Baby Boomers are those born between 1946 and 1964
- Boomers represent a population of 79 million adults
  - Approximately 40% of the USA adult population
  - Controlling over half of the country's wealth ($2+ Trillion)
- Boomers represent the most important market segment for many product categories.

Economic Importance of Boomers
- Boomers control half of the nation's wealth
- 60% are college educated
- Have above average household incomes
- Most important market segment for many product categories

	Older Boomers (1946-55)	Younger Boomers (1956-64)	Total
Spending Power	$1 Trillion	$1.1 Trillion	$2.1 Trillion
% Total USA	24	26	50
% w/College Degree	62	58	60
Avg. People/HH	2.7	3.3	3.0
Avg.Income/HH	$59K	$57K	$58K
# of HH (MM)	21.9	23.9	45.8
Spending Index v. US			
Housing	103	112	108
Transportation	110	124	117
Food	99	120	105
Health Care	129	100	115
Entertainment	108	113	112
Apparel & Svs.	90	124	112
Education	87	200	144

Source: Census, TVB

Media Behavior of Boomers

- Boomers are traditional media junkies, but use all media
  - Television- primetime, news & information, sports
  - Radio – select formats like news/talk, sports, oldies, classic rock, etc.
  - Newspapers – heaviest reader group
  - Magazines – over 50% heavier readers than Gen Y; largest circulation magazine in America is AARP, a group to which older Boomers most likely belong
  - Internet – Use heavily but at a lower rate than Gen Y

- Reportedly get news from advertising from
  - Television – 31%
  - Newspapers – 19%
  - Radio – 19%
  - Internet – 15%
  - Magazines – 2%

- Internet Usage Behavior
  - 69% use the internet on a daily basis
  - Use internet like other users
    - Research products (81% of users)
    - 70% to buy goods
    - 68% to make travel reservations
    - 55% for banking
    - 43% for video sharing
    - 39% social media

- Advertising Media Behavior
  - Use traditional media
  - Use online media

Multi – Cultural Overview

Population Trends

- The face of America is changing. By 2025, nearly 40% of the US population will be minorities, and by 2050, over 50% of the population will be minorities.

- Marketers who currently underperform with minorities will likely lose share as minority markets grow, unless successful market development efforts are undertaken.

	% USA Population	
	1999	**2025**
White Only*	71.9	62.0
Black	12.1	12.9
Hispanic	11.5	18.2
Asian/Other	4.5	7.0

Excludes whites of Hispanic origin. **Includes American Indians, Pacific Islanders, Eskimos, etc. Source: Population Reference Bureau

- The growth of ethnic populations is one of the major marketing trends of the 21st century. Some marketers will benefit from this trend, while others will be adversely affected. Every business, however, should make an informed judgment on whether and how to address the trend. Below is a table describing the projected buying power of ethnic markets (in billions of dollars).

Economic Import of Ethnic Markets

Ethnic Buying Power (B)				
	1990	**2000**	**2008**	**2013**
African Amer.	318	590	913	1,239
Hispanic	212	489	951	1,386
Asian American	117	269	509	752.
Total	4,270	7,188	10,721	14,014

African American (AA) Market

AA Population
- Total AA population estimated at 40+ million in 2010
- Growing faster than total population

Market Segment	1990	2000	2005	2010E	2025E
African Americans (MM)	30	36	38	40	47
AA Index	100	120	127	133	157
Total Population Index	100	113	118	124	162

Demographics

	2005	2006	2007	2008
Median HH Size	NA	2.7	2.7	2.7
HH Income	$31.0	$32.5	$34.2	NA
Any College	NA	NA	NA	40%

Top 15 African American Markets (DMAs)
- AAs highly concentrated in certain DMAs (index > 100):

DMA	% US HH	% AA HH	Cume % AA	AA Index to USA
New York	Los	9.9	9.9	211
Chicago	3.1	4.6	14.4	148
Washington DC	2.0	4.1	18.6	205
Atlanta	1.9	4.0	22.6	211
Philadelphia	2.7	3.9	26.5	144
Los Angeles	5.0	3.7	30.2	74
Detroit	1.8	3.0	33.2	167
Houston	1`.7	2.4	35.6	141
Dallas/FW	2.1	2.3	37.9	110
Baltimore	1.0	2.2	40.1	220
Miami/FL	1.4	2.1	42.2	150
Raleigh/Durham	.9	2.0	44.2	222
Memphis	.6	1.9	46.1	317
Norfolk	.6	1.7	47.8	283
Cleveland	.4	1.6	49.4	114

African American Media

- African Americans can be reached in general market or African American media, e.g.:
  - **Television**: Above average television viewers, especially M-F daytime, sports, programs featuring Black talent, as well as Black Entertainment Television (BET) and others
  - **Radio**: Most major markets have many radio stations programmed for Black audiences
  - **Print**: Leading Black magazines include Ebony, Jet, Essence, Black Enterprise.
  - **Newspapers**: Over 250 Black newspapers located throughout the U.S.
  - **Internet**: African Americans can be reached on the internet:
    - Average time spent online : 18 hours per week
    - Internet access via PC : 93%
    - Internet access via mobile phone : 76%
    - Social Networkers : 50%
    - Avid downloaders of digital content : 66%

Some African American Advice To Ad People

"When you do the common things in life in an uncommon way, you will command the attention of the world."

- George Washington Carver

Asian American Market

Definition

- The Asian American Market includes people defined in terms of countries and regions of origin, language, and cultural characteristics.

Population

- Asian Americans are the fastest growing population segment in the USA, almost 3x faster than the total US population
- Asian American population is projected at over 23 million in 2010 and 28 million by 2025, over 5% of the total U.S. population

Market Segment	1990	2000	2005	2010E	2025E
Asians (MM)	7	18	20	23	28
Asian Index	100	257	286	324	400
Total Population Index	100	113	118	124	162

Demographics

- Over 75% of Asian Americans are foreign born
- More than 78% speak their disputative native languages at home
- Asian Americans are the highest income and best educated ethnic group in the U.S.

Top 15 Asian American Markets (DMAs)

DMA	% US HH	% Asian HH	Cume % AA	Asian Index to USA
Los Angeles	5.0	15.3	15.3	306
New York	6.8	12.9	28.2	190
San Francisco	2.3	11.0	39.2	478
Honolulu	.4	5.0	44.2	1250
Chicago	3.1	3.8	48.0	123
Seattle/Tacoma	1.6	3.3	51.3	206
Sacramento	1.2	3.0	54.3	250
Philadelphia	2.7	2.8	57.1	103
Houston	1.7	2.4	59.5	141
Boston	2.2	2.4	61.9	109
Dallas/FW	2.1	2.4	64.3	114
San Diego	.9	2.3	66.6	256
Atlanta	1.8	2.3	68.9	128
Detroit	1.8	1.6	70.5	89
Minneapolis	1.5	1.4	71.9	93

Asian American Media

- Because of the great diversity in countries of origin, languages and culture, Asian Americans are more difficult to reach and effectively communicate with than most other market segments.

- The minority of Asians who use English as their primary language can be reached in English language media—television, radio, magazines, newspapers, etc. The challenge is greater to reach Asians who have not integrated into the U.S. culture and have not learned good English.

- To reach Asian Americans who speak little English, advertisers must utilize selective media which communicate in the audiences' native languages, including cable TV programs, radio, and print media.

Old Chinese Proverb for Ad People
"To talk much and arrive nowhere
is the same as climbing a tree
to catch a fish."

USA Hispanic Market

Population

- Hispanics currently account for 15% of the USA population
- Hispanics represent the majority of the population in some DMAs
- Hispanics already make up about 60% of the population of San Antonio, TX, and
- Will make up 78 percent of Texas' population growth between now and 2040

Hispanic Population Growth

Market Segment	1990	2000	2005	2010E	2025E
Hispanics (MM)	22	36	38	40	68
Hispanic Index	100	164	173	182	309
Total Population Index	100	113	118	124	162

U.S. Hispanic Demographics

Demographic	USA Hispanics
Median Age	25
White	94%
Black	4%
Immigrant, Fluent English	7
Born in US, Fluent English	88
Country of Origin:	
Mexico	65
Cuba	4
Puerto Rico	9
South America	17
Other	5

Top 15 Hispanic Markets (DMAs)

DMA	% US HH	% Hisp. HH	Cume % Hisp.	Hisp. Index to USA
Los Angeles	5.0	16.0	16.0	320
New York	6.7	11.3	27.3	169
Miami/FL	1.4	5.5	32.8	393
Houston	1.7	4.0	36.8	235
Chicago	3.1	4.0	40.8	129
Dallas/FW	2.1	3.3	44.1	157
S. Fran/O/SJ	2.2	3.3	47.4	150
San Antonio	.7	3.2	50.6	457
Phoenix	1.5	2.5	53.1	167
Harlingen	.3	2.3	55.4	767
Albuquerque	.6	2.1	57.5	350
San Diego	.9	2.0	59.5	222
Sacramento	1.2	1.9	61.4	158
El Paso	.3	1.9	63.3	693
Fresno	.5	1.9	65.2	380

Hispanic Media

- Hispanics may be reached in English language or Spanish language media.

Hispanic Television

- 95% coverage of US Hispanic population
- Univision is the primary television network
- Telemundo is also a major player, plus independent stations
- Programming primarily entertainment, sports, news, novella
- Spots may be purchased on a network or local market spot

Hispanic Radio

Station	Owner	Listeners (M)
KLVE/LA	Univision	2375
WSKQ/NY	Spanish Broadcasting	2328
WSCA/LA	Univision	1774
WPAT/NY	Spanish Broadcasting	1567
KLAX/LA	Spanish Broacastomg	1535

Hispanic Magazines

Magazine	Audience	Circulation (000)	Cost P4C (000)
People en Espanol	Dual	562	$64.5
Latina	Women	500	38.0
Ser Padres	Parents	720	74.8
TV y Novelas	Dual	175	14.7
Vanidades	Women	171	16.5
Selecciones Digest	Dual	381	37.5
Siempre Mujer	Women	419	35.3
Mira	Dual	120	14.4
Hispanic Business (Eng.)	Business	271	19.9

Leading Hispanic Newspapers

Newspaper	Frequency	Circulation	Cost/Inch
El Nuevo Herald/Miami	Daily	164	$32
La Opinion/LA	Daily	286	90
La Raza/Chicago	Weekly	198	NA
Hoy/LA	Daily	420	NA
La Voz/Phoenix	2x/wk	117	NA
La Prensa de San Antonio	Weekly	123	NA
La Opinion Contigo/LA	Weekly	260	NA

Outdoor

- Outdoor can be used to target Hispanics where they live and travel
- Clear Channel Outdoor sells Hispanic showings of varying TRP levels.

Internet

- Over 20 million Hispanics in the USA use the internet
- Use both Spanish and English
- English preferred by majority of internet users

Unique Visitors/Language Preferences

Web Exposure	All Hispanics	English & Spanish	Prefer Spanish	Prefer English
Google Sites	17.5	4.9	4.0	8.6
Yahoo Sites	16.7	4.7	3.8	8.1
Microsoft	14.5	4.3	3.9	6.5
Fox Interactive	11.3	3.5	2.7	5.0
Total Visitors	60.0	174	144	28.1
% Total	100.0	29.0	24	47

Typical Questions

- Upscale Hispanics are fluent in English. "Can we reach the upscale Hispanics we want to reach through our normal general market media buys? Or must we use Hispanic media?"
- "What do we really gain in engagement and relationship building by using Spanish language media?" "Can we use a generic Spanish accent to communicate effectively with those of Mexican, Cuban,

Puerto Rican, and Central/South American descent? Consensus?"
(Answer: yes)

Ad Spending in Hispanic Media

- Total spending fairly flat. 2008 vs. 2007
- Internet spending the one big winner

Expenditures in Hispanic Media, 2008

	2008	% Ch. Vs. 2007
Network TV	$1807	+1
Local TV	707	<1+
National Radio	222	2
Local Radio	529	+1
National Newspapers	124	-
Local Newspapers	186	-
Internet	226	+25
Magazines	115	+4
Out of Home	87	+2
Total	**$4004**	**+1**

A Little Hispanic Wisdom
For Ad People
"Bonitas non est pessimis esse meliorem."
It is not goodness to be better than the worst.

Appendix

Glossary

ABC – Audit Bureau of Circulation. Audits the circulation figures claimed by print media

ADS – Alternative Delivery System to wired cable such as satellite

Arbitron – Leading media research company which measures radio audiences and performs custom research.

AQH – Average Quarter Hour rating.

AA – Average Audience rating. The average number or percentage of homes of persons viewing during the average minute.

Bandwidth – Capacity of communication line to carry information.

Behavioral Targeting (BT) – target an audience by their surfing habits

Blog – Short for Web Log. Online journal or newsletter, frequently updated.

BPA – Business Publications Audit. Company which verifies the circulation of business and trade publications.

Broadband – Transmission frequency which supports wide frequency range.

B/W – Black and white print ads.

Cable TV – Television programming distributed to subscribing households though cables.

Circulation – In print media, the number of copies printed and distributed.

Cost per Acquisition – Payment model paying "X" for sales or inquiry.

Contextual Targeting (CT) – Target ad to specific kinds of content

Cost per Click – In paid internet search, the amount advertisers agree to pay for a click through to their web site.

Cost per Point –Broadcast cost to reach 1% of a universe such as total US households.

CPC – Abbreviation for Cost per Click.

CPM – Cost per Thousand circulation or impressions. CPM = Cost/Audience x 1000. Used to compare the cost efficiency of media vehicles.

CPP – Abbreviation for Cost per Point.

Cume – Cumulative audience, e.g., 1 issue might reach 5% of a target while 4 issues might cume to 10% of the target.

Digital Outdoor Board – High impact digital/electronic board permitting running copy changes.

Direct Marketing – Any marketing activity which sells direct to the consumer via print ads, broadcast, direct mail, telemarketing, etc.

DMA – Designated Market Area (Nielsen defines 211 different DMAs).

DSL – Digital Subscriber Line, filters out noise, connects at higher speed.

Fixed Position – a broadcast spot purchased to run in a particular program and time. Not subject to normal pre-emption policies.

Frequency – The average number of times an audience is reached by media vehicles.

FTP – File Transfer Protocol, method to move files to a server.

GRP – Gross Rating Point, equal to reaching 1% of a universe.

HUTS/PUTS – Percentage of households or persons watching TV or listening to radio at a particular day/time.

Impressions – Number of gross (duplicated) exposures to one or more media vehicles.

Marketing Services Media – Media beyond traditional advertising such as trade & consumer promotion, product placement, event marketing, direct marketing, etc.

Mediamark (MRI) – A leading single source marketing/media research company.

MPA – Magazine Publishers Association, a trade organization promoting magazines.

NAA – Newspaper Advertising Association, a trade organization promoting the use of newspapers.

Nielsen Media Research – The leading media research company which measures network and local market television audiences (ratings).

Open Rate – In print the highest rate against which discounts are based. Usually applies if very few insertions are planned.

Opt In – Individuals who request to be included on certain email lists to receive a newsletter or other information.

Opt Out – Individuals request that their name and email address be eliminated from an email list. :"Do not send me more emails!"

P4C/P2C/PB/W – abbreviation for coloration of ads: page four-color, page two color, page black and white.

Paid Inclusion – Pay search engine to include URL near the top of their listings.

Pay per Action – Ad payment model where a website visitor must not only click on the URL link but must also make a purchase or request information (take an action).

Pay per Click (PPC) – Same as Cost per Click.

Poster (outdoor) – Outdoor board found on main streets in metro areas,

Pre Roll Video – Short clip that plays prior to the selected video smaller than a bulletin, usually printed on paper.

RAB – Radio Advertising Bureau, a trade organization promoting the use of radio for advertising.

Rate Base – Guaranteed circulation for a given advertising rate

Rate Card – A document produced by media which details their advertising rates, discount structures, materials requirements, etc.

Rating – Percentage of a universe viewing or listening to a media vehicle at a particular time.

Rating = Share x HUTS – Formula for calculating or projecting a rating.

Reach – The number or percentage of different target audience persons exposed 1+ times to media vehicles carrying ad message.

Rich Media – Advanced technology used in internet ads to create special effects, streaming video, interactive features.

ROI – Return on Investment.

ROP – Run of paper; print publication places ad where they have open space.

ROS – Run of Schedule, broadcast media run commercial in random positions, not in specified programs.

Rotary Bulletin – Large outdoor board which rotates through a variety of locations. Usually cheaper than permanent bulletin in prime location.

Scatter – Short term broadcast buys made after up front market is over.

Search Engine Marketing (SEM) – Also called paid search. Involves bidding on key words. When people search the key words, your ad may be displayed by the search engine. People who click on your ad are redirected to your website.

Share – The percentage of people who are currently viewing/listening who are tuned to a particular program.

Slotting Fees – Special fees chains may charge marketers in exchange for distribution and shelf space.

SMSA – Standard Metropolitan Statistical Area ("metro area").

Social Media – Media functioning through social interaction, e.g., Facebook.

Street Furniture – out of home advertising on benches and other "furniture."

TRP = Target Rating Point (1% of a target universe).

TVB – Television Bureau of Advertising, an industry organization which promotes the use of television for advertising.

Unique Visitor –Unique IP addresses visiting website for first time.

URL – Uniform Resource Locator (web address)

Reach and Frequency Estimator

- The following reach and frequency table provides general benchmarks. Actual reach and frequency will affected by the particulars of the media plan and how the buy is executed.
- For example, if a television plan consists of a sponsorship of one or two programs, reach may be lower and frequency may skyrocket because a fairly loyal audience is reached over and over.

TRPS:	100	150	200	300	400	500
	R/F	R/F	R/F	R/F	R/F	R/F
Television						
Prime	56/2	60/3	70/3	76/4	80/5	83/6
Early Eve.	48/2	56/3	63/3	66/5	68/6	70/7
Late Eve.	38/3	46/3	52/4	53/6	54/7	55/9
M-F Day	37/3	43/3	49/4	51/6	53/7	55/9
Early/Late	55/2	63/3	68/3	70/4	72/6	74/7
Mix	63/1+	72/2	76/3	80/4	85/5	89/6
Radio						
1 station	15/7	16/9	16/13	17/18	17/24	17/29
3 Stations	30/3	35/4	40/5	45/7	45/9	46/11
10 Stations	66/1	68/2	73/3	76/4	78/5	80/6
Magazines						
Mass/News	40/2	52/3	63/3	70/4	80/5	81/6
Selective	40/2	52/3	58/3	62/5	63/6	64/8
Equal TRPS						
TV/Radio	57/2	66/2	72/3	75/4	77/5	78/6
TV Mags.	60/1	69/2	79/2	80/4	85/5	87/6
TV/Mag/Rad	65/1	71/2	81/2	85/4	88/5	90/5

Source: 2020 Estimates

Table Reads: 100 TRPS in primetime in a typically diversified buy should reach about 56% of the target an average of almost two times

Impress Clients
With Your
Media Acumen

Get Thumbnail Media Planners
for Your Whole Staff
At Discount Prices!

- Learn More
- Plan Faster
- Buy Better
- Look Smarter
- Get Rewarded

www.ThumbnailMediaPlanner.com

2014 Broadcast Calendar

	M	T	W	T	F	S	S
JAN	30	31	1	2	3	4	5
	6	7	8	9	10	11	12
	13	14	15	16	17	18	19
	20	21	22	23	24	25	26
FEB	27	28	29	30	31	1	2
	3	4	5	6	7	8	9
	10	11	12	13	14	15	16
	17	18	19	20	21	22	23
MAR	24	25	26	27	28	1	2
	3	4	5	6	4	5	6
	10	11	12	13	14	15	16
	17	18	19	20	21	22	23
	24	25	26	27	28	29	30
APR	31	1	2	3	4	5	6
	7	8	9	10	11	12	13
	12	13	14	15	16	17	18
	21	22	23	24	25	26	27
MAY	28	29	30	1	2	3	4
	5	6	7	8	9	10	111
	12	14	15	16	17	18	19
	19	20	21	22	23	24	25
	26	27	28	29	30	31	1
JUN	2	3	4	5	6	7	8
	9	10	11	12	13	14	15
	16	18	19	20	21	22	23
	23	24	25	26	27	28	29

Broadcast Calendar 2014

	M	T	W	T	F	S	S
JUL	30	1	2	3	4	5	6
	7	8	9	10	11	12	13
	14	15	16	17	18	19	20
	21	22	23	24	25	26	27
	28	29	30	31	1	2	3
AUG	4	5	6	7	8	9	10
	11	12	13	14	15	16	17
	18	19	20	21	22	23	24
	25	26	27	28	29	30	31
SEP	1	2	3	4	5	6	7
	8	9	10	11	12	13	14
	15	16	17	18	19	20	21
	22	23	24	25	26	27	28
OCT	29	30	1	2	3	4	5
	6	7	8	9	10	11	12
	13	14	15	16	17	18	19
	20	21	22	23	24	25	26
	27	28	29	30	31	1	2
NOV	3	4	5	6	7	8	9
	10	11	12	13	14	15	16
	17	18	19	20	21	22	23
	24	25	26	27	28	29	30
DEC	1	2	3	4	5	6	7
	8	9	10	11	12	13	14
	15	16	17	18	19	20	21
	22	23	24	25	26	27	28
	29	30	31	1	2	3	4

Media Management Check List

Marketing Situation
✓ Understand the marketing situation, including...
✓ Marketing Objectives & Strategies
✓ Consumer/target segmentation
✓ Geographic business analysis
✓ Purchase Behavior
✓ Problems and Opportunities

Media Objectives
✓ Based on the marketing situation, define the media objectives:
✓ Who, where, when, how much

Media Strategy
✓ Based on the media objectives, develop the optimal media strategies to address each objective

Tactical Plan
✓ Develop and execute the most cost effective tactics in relation to each strategy
✓ Vehicle selection, scheduling, geographic weighting, budgets

Buying Specs
✓ Provide accurate direction to the buyers so that the plan can be optimally executed, quantitatively and qualitatively

Performance
✓ Evaluate the plan in relation to the media objectives prior to buy
✓ Evaluate the plan vs. actual buy and results

Improvement
✓ Identify learnings and how to improve the planning and buying process in your organization.
✓ Monitor & diagnose performance

Media Contacts

COMPANY	NAME	PHONE

Thank you for purchasing the *2014 Thumbnail Media Planner...* we hope it was helpful to you.

We leave you with some advice for success in with clients in the highly competitive advertising business.

> **"Always do more**
>
> **than is required of you."**
>
> --General George S. Patton. Jr.

CPSIA information can be obtained at www.ICGtesting.com
Printed in the USA
BVOW02s1959290815

415723BV00014B/260/P

9 781493 590254